Speedwriting

the international ABC shorthand

DICTATION COURSE

SPEEDWRITING LIMITED,

59–60–61 SOUTH MOLTON STREET

LONDON W1Y 2AX

NOTICE

You are now studying a course in "SPEEDWRITING", a name which identifies the most efficient system of ABC shorthand. It is known throughout the world by the distinguishing trade mark "SPEEDWRITING".

ISBN 0 905480 20 1

Reprinted 1974
Reprinted 1975
Reprinted 1976

Printed in Great Britain by A. Wheaton & Co. Exeter

CONTENTS

GENERAL INDEX

INTRODUCTION

This speed course is especially designed for the SPEED-WRITING SHORTHAND WRITER. It incorporates the salient features of the 'Dictation Course' published by the Speedwriting Company of New York.

It cannot be too strongly emphasized that the acquisition of outlines for new words is the primary need. If the writer secures a large vocabulary, which can be instinctively written by habit, not only does the writing of those words become effortless, but other outlines for words never written before are more quickly formed in the mind of the writer.

To work alone is best for this.

In one piece of dictation, for example, a student may find he has to practise six words because the outlines are unfamiliar, whereas another student in the same class may need practice on six quite different words. It follows, therefore, that individual study provides for progress in vocabulary building. This book is designed to help you in this individual study.

When a piece is given in dictation, it is counted in groups of 20 words.

The book is divided into sections as follows:
   A. Simple Dictation
   B. Vocabulary Increase
   C. Practices from the Dictionary
   D. General Dictation
   E. Business English
   F. Transcription Technique

It is not intended that this book should be worked through consecutively by the student. It is best, for instance, for sections A, B and C to be used concurrently.

The reader is referred to the introduction of each section.

SIMPLE DICTATION

The object of this section is to help the student who emerges from the mastery of theory to the work of a speed class. Each piece of dictation has a word list, which the student should master first. Then he, or she, is ready for dictation of the following text matter.

Be thorough in your practices. Make the words come by *habit* not *memory*. The difference between 'habit' and 'memory' is just this—

' You want to catch a bus, so your legs move more quickly. You do not have to think 'left-right, left-right' faster! That shows that running is an act of *habit*.

Now apply that principle to shorthand.

When someone says a word or words, the writing of it is automatic; it is thoughtless.

How do we get habits? Habits—good or bad—are secured by repetition, that is, doing things over and over again. If you tell your hand to write words or sentences again and again it will know what to do instinctively.

Apply yourself to this repetition practice.

The aim of this section is manual dexterity. The words being completely elementary (one or two syllables), no word list is needed. Phrasing and condensed notes are to be specially observed in students' notebooks.

Without a word list preceding, the pupil has to make his or her own attempt at outlines.
Check carefully with the dictionary.
Practise corrections, if any, and re-dictate at higher speed.

1

There is such a lot you can do with shorthand. You may think that it is of use only to / find a job that you must do to earn a 40 living. You would be surprised at the people who do // not *need* to earn a living who learn shorthand. If you only knew . . .

For example, you want to remind yourself / of something. The back of an old envelope will do. You think of something 80 you want to tell someone, you // have a letter to write or things occur to you at odd moments. If you jot them down they will / not be forgotten when you write. A speech has to be made and 120 you have to make it. No one // leaves points that will interest the hearers to the moment of speaking. Jot them down in shorthand.

If some of / you would like to teach, here is something that 160 will readily give you an opportunity. Try an evening class in // shorthand—there is always an opening.

Now that Speedwriting has come to Britain there is more demand for teachers than / ever. Every business man and woman who wants shorthand can now learn it easily. There is 200 no shorthand so simple // to learn and so well adapted to our everyday needs. Let people know that you can teach them.

2

It is rather exciting being able to do what other people cannot do. This is what you are in the / shorthand class to learn. You can now do more than many people, but you want to get a 40 speed that // other people wish they could get but cannot. You really will feel that your time spent in your last year / at school has been worth while.

Other people may do some things easily that you cannot do. 80 They may be // good at figures or knitting, good at tennis, good at skating—and you may not be so good. Whichever it / is, it did not come in a moment. These people had to learn and 120 practise week after week before they became better // than others. So you in your line have had to practise and practise over and over again to become an / expert at shorthand—fluent and fast.

3

Homework is a difficult thing to talk about. Home is home and work is work. They do not seem to / mix. Home is where we do what we like and work is what we do only because we must. Your // homework shows your teacher that you like the subject   40 or that you do it only because you must.

You like / what is going to bring you money to buy things you want—dresses, holidays, dances.

In the long run your // homework is going to help bring you   80 money for these things. Therefore it would be wise to like your homework! /

If you do homework only because you must, you will do the minimum work in your job—and for the // minimum pay, too.   120

If your boss asks "Do you enjoy your work?" and you say "No", you might be dismissed! / Make your answer a truthful "Yes". If he says "Would you enjoy a better post?" what would you say? Let // it be a truthful "Yes" again.   160

The wish to 'get on' is all very well, but you can reach journey's / end only by making the journey. So make up your mind to stay the course whatever it entails. The rough // parts of the   200 road will not last always. Show that for a time you can make yourself do what you / do not like. Brighter days will come.

4

When you write the word 'short' and the word 'hand' you learn how to join them so as to make / one word—'shorthand'. This gives you an idea. Many long words are composed of two short ones, so that if // you make sure of short words you will   40 be able to take a great number of long ones in your / notes without delay.

I can give you more examples of this. Why not join 'hand' and 'bag' to make 'handbag'? // Also the brief form 'out' and   80 the word 'fit' for 'outfit' is easy, and, again, 'text' and 'book' make 'textbook'— / but perhaps you know this already. You can think of many others for yourselves.

This will show you how necessary // it is to know well the   120 basic rules in the early chapters of your textbook. Really, shorthand is easy. What / you have learnt makes it easy for you. In

160 any calling in life, and whatever you do, to make quick // notes
is a great asset. Though you may not all become secretaries, you
183 will never regret the shorthand you have / learnt at school.

5

You will find that words grow out of one another. You have
found already that two words together often make / one long
one. Now I want to show you that by adding letters one word
40 will grow into many others. //

If you can write the word 'pen', you will not find it hard to
write 'pens', and 'pence'. The outlines / are quite different. Now
you can write 'pencil' and I think you can write 'dispense',
'expense', 'suspense'.

80 Take the word // 'stand'. We can make other words from it.
Write the words 'withstand', 'understand', 'standard', 'stand-
point'. Your teacher will correct your / outlines.

See what we can make out of 'able'. From this word come:

table	sable	fable
gable	suitable	returnable
receivable	reachable //	curable
ability	readable	notable

120

You can think of other words that will grow into a big family
of words, / all with one common syllable. There is another from
143 'able'—the word 'syllable'. When you have thought of a list //
like this learn the right outline for each one and practise it.

6

Dear Sirs,

We are in receipt of your letter of the 14th instant about the
exercise books recently delivered to / you. We are naturally
very sorry indeed that such an unfortunate mistake should have
40 been made, and assure you of // our intention to put the matter
right with the least possible delay. The books were sent to you
immediately they / were received from the printers, and, in fact,
were dispatched without our having an opportunity of examin-
80 ing them before they // left the premises. We note that you have
returned the consignment to us, and on receipt we shall ask the /
printers to replace the present covers with new ones.

Covers will correspond with the ruling inside the books.

120 It is, // we admit, very annoying that you should receive a consignment of cash books marked on the cover as ledgers, espe-

4

cially / as delivery had been so considerably delayed. Any expenses incurred by you will be deducted from your account.

We have // been in touch with the suppliers and they ask us to   160
offer you their apologies and to give their assurance / that every effort will be made to return the books to you as soon as possible.

We thank you for // your enquiry concerning the printing of   200
programmes. We are in a position to undertake the work and to guarantee delivery / within the time specified in your letter. An estimate will be sent to you during // the next few days.

Yours // faithfully,   240

(Examination paper, Royal Society of Arts.)

7

It is a fairly easy and normal matter to arrange for men to move our goods from one house to / another. Everyone does it. But it is surprising to find that in America there are at least a thousand firms // which will undertake to move the house as   40
well! One firm buys houses to be moved and takes them to / its grounds where they are sold like used cars at prices that include delivery.

Sometimes, one wing of a house // is moved to one place and   80
the remainder to another. Often, large houses are turned into two smaller ones by / removing the top storey.

8

Dear Sir,

As you have probably read in our local press, one result of new Town Planning Orders, as well / as schemes for the construction of a new motor road, will be that our present shop premises will be due // for demolition in the near future. We   40
have considered very carefully the question of our removal to new premises and / in view of the very large stocks we carry, we feel we should be well advised to sell the whole // of our   80
goods on the spot. To avoid the cost of removal, we have reduced the price of every article, / some by as much as 50 per cent, and we invite you to take advantage of this opportunity.

(Examination paper, Royal Society of Arts.)

There are a great many words that change only the first letter or syllable, while the other part is the / same. This makes it very easy to make one word out of another. Here are some simple ones.

40   bind   mind // find   kind   rind   wind
            dust   rust   crust   trust   must

From these words you can easily make a great number of / other words if you want to. The word 'kind' turns into 'kindly'
80 'kindness' 'unkind'; and the word 'rust' will become // 'rusty' 'rusting' 'rusted' 'thrust' 'rustic'.

If you think of those word families you will really help yourself, and if you / can at once write 'kind' or 'rust' you are ready
120 when any word developed from it is dictated to you. //

A very important day in your life is coming—the day you apply for your first post. To some people / who are shy about it
40 it is no use at such a time to say, 'Don't panic'. You may think // you never would. Do not be too sure; the nearer that day comes the bigger it seems.

There is no / reason why you should not enjoy it, so let me tell you something of what it is like.
80 First of // all, don't be sad if you do not get the first post you apply for. Do not think to yourself / 'I *must* get it'. That gives you a 'driven' feeling, just as it is silly to enter an examination
120 thinking // 'I *must* pass'. You want to be at ease, to show your best points. To be at your best do / your utmost to show your real self—not what you suppose your employer would like.
160 Be keen. Keen to help, // keen to oblige, keen to get on with people, keen to answer all questions.

Dress just as you would / if you were in the job; do not dress up. The employer may take marks off for this.
200 Think up // two or three questions to ask about the work and ask them before you leave. It shows interest in your / work and
230 will please. Do not appear to know everything.

When you get into your post with the desire to do well in it there are some things you need / to remember always. Of course you will want to do your best in any post you take, because if you // please your employer you will get more money.   40

Be neat. Do not let your desk or your drawers be a / litter of things you want so that you have to look for them. Arrange a place for each thing and // put each thing in its place. Even a   80 rubber or pins or bands—put them where they are easy to / get at so that you do not waste time looking for them.

Be neat, too, in your appearance. This does // not mean 120 wearing dresses that cost a lot. You must be seen, so appear as you like others to appear. / You do not like to see people untidy. No need for costly 'hair-do's'. A comb and brush are all // you need. Use them freely.   160

Be on time in the morning—and again at night leave on time. If you / are not on time at the beginning of the day you hardly deserve to finish on time. You will be // happier; you will not 200 feel 'driven'; work will be easier and the day will seem happier if there is little / or nothing held over from the day before.

How many people tell me they cannot spell! Some of them add 'I never could spell'. Why should they say / that? At one time they could not walk, but they can walk now. Because you cannot do a thing at // one time you must not say you never   40 will do it.

You have only to pay attention in order to / spell. It is nothing more difficult than that. When you come to a word you are not sure // about, look it up and *make* sure, then learn it.   80

To learn it, copy it six times thoughtfully. Spell it / aloud if you want to make quite sure of it. Say it several times.

It only needs attention. Try it. // The more difficult words 120 which you do not come across often you may have to learn specially. There are many / spelling books to help you, and dictionaries too, but pay attention when you read either.

160   You see, suppose you apply // for a job and others are after it too. In making his choice an employer would choose the lady who / can spell better than the others. I would. You would.

200   You would not want spelling mistakes all over your letters. //

So you may find that one day you get the post you want because, although many other people wanted it, / they did not prepare for it as well as you did. You can start to prepare for

240 that job *now*. //

13

When you come across a word you do not know the meaning of, be sure you ask someone or go / to the dictionary to find out. The more words you understand, the more interesting life is.

40 It is like getting // a wider view. You listen to different people and what they say really means something to you.

It works the / other way too. When you talk to other people

80 you can say just what you want to say. You will // not have to say 'What I mean is . . .' and start all over again. So many people have to do this and / they waste a lot of time and are usually not very interesting people to talk to.

As you mix with other // people, learn the words they use and the meaning of them, so that you can use them too when when you talk.

14

Let us see if we can make up a piece to take down with just short words.

There is no need / to use a long word where a short word will

40 do. You can be plain and yet not // use long words. Long words may have to be used to give the real thoughts we want to say. If you had a dog and you were very fond of it you would call it

80 a 'pet' but one who does // not like dogs might call it a 'cur'. But to be more plain as to the kind of dog it / was you would of course have to give the name of the breed. That would make

120 clear what it looked // like, its shade, its coat, its size. If you use

138 a long word it may be more descriptive.

(The only word of more than one syllable is the last.)

VOCABULARY INCREASE

This section is at once informative and repetitive.

You may come across words that are new to you. When you get an opportunity, make it a rule to look them up in an English dictionary and find out what they mean.

If you make a rule to do this in your post, your job will become more and more interesting.

There are many people who are not highly educated, who are well-informed. It is more practically useful to be well-informed; though, of course, you may be both.

Do not let experience slip through your fingers.

Be intent on understanding all you hear. Even these exercises are designed to increase your general knowledge and therefore your interest in life.

Words must not be learnt as isolated signs, but included with derivatives and words with similar prefixes and suffixes.

1

WORD PRACTICE BEFORE DICTATION

attend	*al —*	listener	*Lsn*
agony	*agn*	stifle	*sfl*
resting	*rs*	swallow	*s—lo*
fingers	*Jgs*	awful	*af*
tightly	*til*	gulp	*glp*
possibility	*psb)*	emotional	*e—yl*
speaker	*Sk*	longer	*Lg*
intervals	*Nvls*	continue	*Ku*
sooner	*Sn*	causes	*kzs*
later	*La*	creep	*kep*

DICTATION

If you attend a dinner and have to suffer the agony of an after-dinner speech, do not sit with your / head resting on your hands unless the fingers of one hand are tightly holding the
40 fingers of the other, for // if you should fall asleep there is every possibility that your hands will fall apart and your chin will hit / the table. Always grip the table and gaze at the speaker, nodding at intervals.
80 Sooner or later, every listener must // face the problem of how to stifle a yawn. I do not recommend you to swallow, because the sound produced— / that awful gulp—will probably be heard. Neither is it wise to try to stop it, for the effort

10

causes // the eyes to run, and if the speaker is telling an emo- 120
tional story he thinks he has touched you and / makes the story
even longer. Easily the best policy is to drop something under
the table and whilst on hands // and knees get rid of the yawn 160
safely, then continue to creep on all fours out of the room.

(Examination paper, Council of West Riding of Yorkshire.)

2

WORD PRACTICE BEFORE DICTATION

realising	*rlz*	opportunities	*opls*
accidents	*xd --*	brakes	*bks*
narrow	*nro*	figures	*fgs*
winding	*r --*	proportion	*ppf*
temptations	*ulys*	crimes	*kis*
abreast	*ab,*	constantly	*ks-l*
authorities	*a))*	worst	*r,*
corners	*Kns*	blind	*bi --*
invitations	*nvlys*	crowding	*k d*
collisions	*klys*	of course	*vks*
selfishness	*s'z'*	stream	*Se*
irritation	*uy*	traffic	*Yfk*
danger	*D1*	as soon as	*sns*

11

dangerous	*ᗞ𝒳ˣ*	refuse	*ɾfʒ*
drivers	*ᗞ𝓊𝓈*	disastrous	*dᴔᔕ𝓇*
cautious	*kᴋ*		

DICTATION

No one can drive on the main roads from London to the north and west without realising the real causes / of so many road accidents.

It is true that many of our roads are narrow and winding,
40 and that many // more of them are what you might call 'temptations'—that is, they are nearly wide enough for three cars abreast / but not quite. It is true that the authorities are still building these real death traps, these roads with three // tracks,
80 which, on corners and hills are open invitations to join in head-on collisions. Still, it is nothing but / pure selfishness that brings the use of them out of irritation and delay into deadly danger.
120 The most dangerous drivers // on the roads today are those who consider themselves good drivers—the men in fast cars. Women drivers are often / slow and over-cautious, but I have
160 yet to see a case of really dangerous driving by a woman. She // will miss a dozen opportunities to pass, but very rarely does she take a dangerous one. If you want to / pass her she will draw in to the side and even put her brakes on. I should very much
200 like // to know the figures for road accidents and to see how many are caused by men and by women in / proportion to the numbers of both using the roads.

Among the road crimes committed constantly, three stand
240 out clearly. The // worst is passing 'blind' on hills and corners. The second is the 'crowding' oh an overtaking car, and this can / bring danger even to a one-way road with two tracks. The
280 last crime, of course is cutting-in. There // is a stream of traffic waiting to pass a lorry. As soon as it is safe every car will pull / out and pass. Some drivers, however, in fast cars, refuse to wait
320 their turn. They pull out with disastrous results. //

(Examination paper, Royal Society of Arts.)

12

WORD PRACTICE BEFORE DICTATION

sales	*sals*	create	*kea*
salesman	*sls —*	creation	*kej*
salesmanship	*sls —3*	big	*bq*
every	*Ev,*	bigger	*Bq*
everyone	*Ev, 1*	biggest	*bq,*
everything	*Ev,*	successful	*suc*
order	*O*	market	*kl*
advertise	*avz*	thorough	*tro*
advertisement	*avz —*	thoroughly	*trol*
public	*pb*	acquaint	*aq —*
publication	*pbj*	acquaintance	*aq*
interest	*N,*	substantial	*ssx*
interesting	*Ns*	substance	*ss*
secure	*sku*	provide	*pvd*
securing	*sku*	provision	*pvj*

security	*sku)*	enjoy	*nyy*
recognize	*rkgnz*	enjoyment	*nyy-*
recognizable	*rkgnzb*	other	*O*
feature	*Jo*	otherwise	*O3*
progress	*pg'*	obtain	*obln*
progressive	*pgsv*	obtainable	*oblnb*
		unobtainable	*uoblnb*

DICTATION

The art of salesmanship is to secure buyers for goods or services. Salesmanship does not consist of selling those things / that people have got to have in order to live. Many forms of 40 publicity are used to bring goods to // the notice of the public who may be interested in them. Salesmanship secures buyers. Salesmanship has come to be recognized / as one of the main features of a progressive business. It secures for a particular 80 business or trade customers for // the goods offered for sale by that business. It may have to create demand. It is perhaps the biggest factor / in successful marketing of goods. Those who work in this field must be thoroughly acquainted with the con-120 ditions of those // to whom they sell.

4

WORD PRACTICE BEFORE DICTATION

different	*df-*	treat	*Ze*
imitate	*cla*	sometimes	*sdus*

happiest	*hp,,*	sports	*s //*
begin	*bg*	friendships	*f — 3s*
another	*aO*	admire	*a n*
certainly	*s/nl*	colleagues	*klgs*
salaries	*slys*	clever	*Kv*
workers	*Uks*	because	*ks*
interesting	*Ns*	explain	*xpn*
inclined	*ncn*	helpful	*hpf*
across	*ak'*	grounds	*gv— —*
longer	*Lg*	facilities	*fsl))*

DICTATION

Your business life is beginning. You will find it very different from school life and very different from home life, / but very interesting.

Look for the interesting parts in it. You will, of course, get paid for what you do— // that will be interesting—and you will **40** meet a lot of people. Some you will like and some you may / not like so much, some you will admire and perhaps imitate, others you will wish to keep away from; but // because you have to **80** work with them, you cannot choose your colleagues.

You will find it the happiest way for / yourself not to think too much about those whom you do not like, or you will get to dislike them // more and more, and that only makes work **120** harder for you.

15

You will come across some very clever people too. / All those people when you begin have been in the firm longer than you 160 have, so make sure you watch // how they do things, because they have found that the best way to do that particular job. If you have / to do that job or another like it, try the way they do 200 it before you try one of your // own.

5

WORD PRACTICE BEFORE DICTATION

printer	*P̲*	correctly	*krkl*
printing	*p=*	incorrect	*nkrk*
printed	*p⁼*	low	*lo*
reprint	*rp–*	lower	*Lo*
composed	*kpz̄*	lowest	*lo,*
composure	*kpz*	produce	*pds*
composing	*kp3–*	product	*pdk*
decompose	*dkp3*	production	*pdkf*
write	*ri*	reproduce	*rpds*
written	*rln*	reproduction	*rpdkf*
unwritten	*urln*	less	*l'*
rewritten	*rrln*	lessen (lesson)	*lsn*

16

typewritten	*tprtn*	lessened	*lsn̄*
refer	*rf*	lessening	*lsn̠*
referred	*rf̄*	care	*ka*
reference	*rf*	careful	*kaf*
suffice	*sfs*	careless	*kal'*
sufficient	*sfz-*	carelessly	*kalsl*
sufficiently	*sfz-l*	fault	*flt*
render	*R—*	faulty	*flt,*
paper	*Pp*	faultless	*fltl'*
interest	*n,*	prescribe	*pskb*
interested	*n̄s*	prescribed	*pskb̄*
interesting	*ns̠*	style	*sl*
author	*a*	styles	*sls*
authority	*a)*	stylish	*slz*
legible	*lgb*	faithfully	*ff*
matter	*na*	public	*pb*
material	*nal*	publicly	*pbl*

17

materially *ℓal*   publish *pb*

correct *krk*   publishing *pb*

corrections *krkjs*

DICTATION

The matter supplied to a printer is to be set up or composed. It may be written by hand, typewritten / or ordinary print. This is generally referred to as 'copy' and it should be sufficiently
40 legible to render the work // of setting up as easy as possible, being written on one side of the paper only. It is in the / interest of the author to provide the printer with legible 'copy', as it
80 materially reduces the cost of composing and // corrections, thus securing a lower price for the work. In a reprint of printed matter the cost of production is / greatly lessened over new work.

When the 'copy' has been carelessly prepared, perhaps by a
110 writer who spells incorrectly, it // is the duty of the printer to correct these faults according to the style prescribed by the office in which / he works, but when copy has been carefully prepared
140 by a writer who has a style of his own, that // copy should be followed faithfully. It is the author's right to go before the
164 public in his own way and / in his own style.

6

WORD PRACTICE BEFORE DICTATION

hardly *h/ℓ*   director *Drk*

concerned *ksñ*   usual *x*

active *akv*   unusual *ux*

18

over and over again	*Waq*	wonder	*U—*
		wondered	*U—=*
urgently	*uy-l*	convenient	*kvn—*
o'clock	*oklk*	inconvenient	*nkvn—*
brood	*vd*	inconvenience	*nkv/*
lately	*lal*	alter	*al*
another	*aO*	altered	*al*
unending	*ue—=*	alteration	*aly*
ending	*e—=*	alternative	*alnv*
change	*cy*	wait	*ᴗa*
changing	*cy_*	waiter	*Ua*
changeable	*cyb*	waiting	*ᴗa*
straw	*Sa*		

DICTATION

Betty was waiting. She was not very clear what she was waiting for. That did not worry her much. Why / she was told to
wait hardly concerned her. If the truth were known, what was
going through her active brain // was the work that had piled .40
up at her desk that remained to be done, and over and over
again / she thought about those jobs, some urgently needed.

The time was just past 4 o'clock and all those things that // 80
had to be done made her brood; she hated to let people down.
Things had become more and more pressing / lately; she never

19

got away on time and that was not because she was slow. She
120 knew her work and // did it well, but more and more was put
upon her. She could not keep taking on one job after / another.
It seemed quite unending. In fact she had even thought of
160 changing her job—and now to have to // wait added to her
work, and seemed the last straw.

It was not often she was called to the director's / office, and
because it was unusual she wondered why it had been she, and
200 of all things today, and at // the end of the day. It was incon-
venient, but could not be avoided. There was nothing to do
about it, / so she waited.

Next time I shall tell you what she was waiting for.

7

WORD PRACTICE BEFORE DICTATION

attached	$a\bar{lc}$	spoken	skn
attaching	$a\underset{\sim}{lc}$	parents	pr--
attachment	$alc-$	accommodate	akda
director	Drk	accommodating	akda
secretary	sec	accommodation	akdy
greet	ge	arrive	rv
greeting	ge	arrival	rvl
greetings	ge	familiar	Jl
cheerful	cef	holiday	hld
afternoon	afn	cloth	kl
noon	n	clothing	kl

20

usual	✗	allow	
unusual	ux	allowance	
accumulation	akly	salary	sly
Singapore	sgpo	confused	kfȝ
wonder	∪—	grumble	g b
wondering	∪=	grumbling	g b
wonderment	∪—-	selfish	s ȝ
abroad	abd	unselfishly	us ȝl
object	ob	interview	nvu
objection	obj	restless	rsl'

DICTATION

Betty Marshall was still sitting in the secretary's office attached to the one the director used. His secretary was there. / Others came through and went out; Betty seemed to be left till the last. Why had they sent for her // so early? She could not   40
help being restless.

Half an hour had gone by.

At last her turn came and / she was asked to go in to the director. She was greeted with a cheerful, 'Good afternoon, Miss Marshall. Please // sit down.' It seemed very unusual to Betty.   80
She expected some notes or another job to add to the accumulation /—as if she had not enough already! She was surprised.

21

120 'I have sent for you, Miss Marshall, to tell you // what is in
my mind so that you can give it due consideration,' he began.
'You may already know I / have to go to Singapore for 3
160 months and expect to be very busy there. I leave in 4 weeks' //
time. It is necessary for me to take the help I need, because good
staff are most difficult to find / there. I have followed your work
in the company over the past 18 months, and I wonder if you
200 have // any objection to going abroad. It will only be for a time
and I have spoken to those for whom / you work at present.
They will find someone else for your duties.
240 'I am going to tell you the conditions. //I want you to consult
your parents and tell me on Wednesday whether you accept.
'Naturally, expenses will be paid, / both travel and accom-
modation in Singapore. I go by sea myself because I have other
280 visits to make on the // way, and I shall arrive on June 20th.
I want you to work here till I leave so that you / can be familiar
with what is happening, then you can have 10 days' holiday and
320 fly out so that you // reach there on June 18th. It may be hot
there in those weeks, so that I have arranged for a / clothing
allowance to be made to you up to £50 to get what you need
360 before you go. There will // be a small addition to your salary.
I think you will enjoy the work.'
Betty was really rather confused. It / was sudden. She was
pleased and proud that she should be chosen; all thought of
400 overwork was gone; the grumbles // she had as she went in were
finished. It was *because* she had worked so hard and unselfishly
that she / had been selected. All her overwork seemed so worth
while now. This was her opportunity.

PRACTICES FROM THE DICTIONARY

These are only a few examples that you may appropriate and expand at your leisure.

If you learn words with the same prefix and practise the shorthand outlines, you will feel on familiar ground when these words are dictated. By the time you have written the prefix your mind will have recalled the outline for the rest of the word.

For instance, two prefixes are 'Inter—' and 'Con—'. Without any list at all you can at this moment write down a dozen or more words beginning with these syllables.

To the list I have made, you can add more; but the prefix is purposely not repeated so that you may think of the rest of the word.

While writing the capital N for 'Inter—' in shorthand all your mind has to do is to form the outline for

> —cept
> —cede
> —sect
> —section
> —lope
> —meddle

In the same way 'Con—' is very common, so that while you write the speedwriting outline of 'k' you will recall how to form

> —fess
> —fuse
> —demn
> —sider
> —cession
> —nect
> —sent
> —sult

and so on.

The list of words may take time, but besides learning the outline the students *must understand what the word means.* The shorthand writer must understand the sense of what is dictated, and time taken by the teacher to ensure this is general education.

Make further tests of your own. Take your dictionary and fill in the correct outlines. Practise one line of each. The following day, cover the outlines and see if you can write them again correctly. Any errors should be given two lines of practice.

PRACTICES FROM THE DICTIONARY

Revise Rule 26. (Hyphen)

ant	anticipate
antagonism	anticipation
antagonist	antidote
antecedent	antipathy
antedated	antiquated
antelope	antique
anterior	antiquity
anteroom	antiseptic

Words beginning with AB—

abandon	abreast
abandonment	abridge
abase	abroad
abasement	abrupt
abate	abruptness

24

abatement	absence
abbreviate	absent
abbreviation	absolute
abeyance	abstain
ability	abstract
able	abstraction
abolish	abundance
abolition	abundant
about	abuse
above	abusive

Words beginning with DE—

debar	deduct
debase	deface
debate	default
debenture	defeat
debit	defect
decamp	defence
decapitate	defend
decay	defiance
deceive	deformity

decent... defraud ....

deception.................................. defray...

decide....................................... defunct.......................................

decision .... degenerate..................................

declaim .... degrade ....

declare..................................... delay...

decline .... delete ....

decompose............................... delight ....

decrease................................... demerit ....

decree....................................... demolish ....

deduce .... demur ....

denude.......................................

More words beginning with DE—

depart .... describe ....

depend................................. desert...

dependent .... deserve.......................................

deplete............................... design..

26

deplore	desire
deport	desirable
depose	desirous
depravity	despair
depress	despise
deprive	despondency
depute	destination
deride	destiny
derive	destitute
descend	

Words beginning with DIS—

disagree	discord
disallow	discourage
disappear	discover
disappoint	discovery
disapprove	discreet
disarrange	discretion

27

disband .... discriminated ....

disburse .... discuss ....

discern .... disdain ....

discernment......................... disengage................................

discipline .... disentangle ....

disclose .... disfigure.................................

discomfort............................. disgrace ....

disconcerted .... disguise ....

disconnect............................. dishonest ....

discontinue ....

More words beinning with DIS—

disinfect................................ displease ....

disjoin .... dispose....................................

dislike .... dispute....................................

dislodge................................ disregard ....

dismember............................ disrepair ....

dismiss.................................. disrespect..............................

28

disobey	disrupt
disorganise	dissatisfaction
disparity	dissent
dispatch	dissipate
dispel	dissolve
dispense	dissuade
dispensation	distance
disperse	distasteful
displace	distend

Words pronounced with distinct sound of E initially—

eclipse	elastic
economy	elate
efface	elect
effacement	election
effective	electric
effectual	electricity
effete	electrify

29

efficiency ....

efficient ....

effulgent ....

effusive ....

egress ....

eject ....

ejection ....

elapse ....

electrode ....

electrolysis ....

eliminate ....

ellipse ....

elusive ....

emerge ....

emit ....

Words beginning with EM—
Rule 53

emanate ....

embalm ....

embark ....

embarrass ....

emblem ....

emboss ....

embrace ....

emperor ....

emphasize ....

emphatic ....

empire ....

employ ....

employer ....

employee ....

30

embroider	empress
emerald	employment
emery	empty
emigrate	emulate
eminent	emulsion

Words beginning with EN—
Rule 36

enable	energy
encamp	enfold
encircle	enforce
enclose	engage
enclosure	engrave
encompass	entrance
encourage	enjoy
encroach	enjoyable
encumber	enlarge
endanger	enlighten
endeavour	enlist

31

endorse .... enormous.....................................

endowment .... enquire.......................................

endure .... enrol...

enemy... ensign.......................................

Words beginning with EX—
Rule 37

exact.. excuse.......................................

exalt.. execute.....................................

examine .... executive ....

example .... exempt......................................

excavate.. exercise ....

excel.. exert...

excellent... exhaust.....................................

except.. exhibit ....

excess.. exhort ....

exchange .... extreme ....

excited .... exile ....

excitement.. exist ....

32

exclude	expanse
exclusive	expect
excursion	expedient

More words beginning with EX—

expedite	expunge
expel	exquisite
expense	extend
expensive	extension
experiment	extent
expert	exterior
expire	external
explain	extinct
explode	extinguish
exploit	extort
explore	extra
export	extract
expose	extraneous

exposure ....

express ....

expressive ....

expulsion ....

extravagance ....

extreme ....

exult ....

Words beginning with IM—
Rule 53

image ....

imagine ....

imbibe ....

immaculate ....

imminent ....

immediate ....

immense..

immerge...

imminence..

immorality...

immune ....

immutable...

impede ....

impel ....

imperative ....

imperfect ....

imperial ....

imperious ....

impersonal ....

implicate ....

imply ....

import ....

important ....

impose ....

34

impact ....

impostor ....

impale ....

impress...................................

impart ....

impulse ....

impatient...................................

Words beginning with IN—(meaning "not")
Rule 36

incomparable ....

indeterminate ....

incomplete...................................

indirect...................................

inconceivable ....

indiscreet...................................

inconsiderate...................................

indistinct ....

inconsistent...................................

ineffable...................................

inconstant ....

inefficient...................................

incorrect ....

inept...................................

incorruptible...................................

inert ....

incredible...................................

inexact ....

indecent...................................

inexcusable ....

indecisive...................................

inexpedient ....

indecorous...................................

inexpensive ....

indefinite .... infallible ....

independence .... infinite ....

indescribable............................. inglorious ....

More words beginning with IN—

inhabit .... inside ....

inhale.................................... insight ....

inherit .... insist....................................

iniquity .... insolent ....

initial .... inspect ....

inject .... inspector ....

injure .... install....................................

injurious .... instance ....

ink .... instead ....

innate.................................... instinct....................................

inner.................................... institute ....

innocent.................................... instructor....................................

inquest.................................... instrument....................................

inquire.. insular ....

insect .... invitation................................

insert ....

Words beginning with MIS—

misapplied............................. mishap................................

misbehave .... misinform ....

misbelieve .... misjudge ....

miscarry................................ mislay ....

miscellaneous .... mismanage ....

mischance .... misplace.............................

mischief............................... misprint..............................

misconduct .... misrepresent ....

misdirect .... missile ....

miserable............................. mistake ....

misfit .... mistress ....

misgiving............................. misunderstand ....

37

Words beginning with OVER—

overbalance..	overlap..
overboard	overlook ....
overcame..	overpower ....
overcharge..	override ....
overcoat..	overseas..
overdrive	oversight ....
overdue	overstrain ....
overflow..	overtake..
overhang	overthrow ....
overhaul..	overtime..
overhear..	overwhelm..
overjoyed..	overturn..
overlaid	overwork..

Words beginning with RE—(meaning "again")

recommence	reform ....
recommit	refresh ....

reconsider	refreshment
recover	regain
recreate	regenerate
recurrence	reimburse
redeem	reinstate
redirect	reinvest
redouble	rejoice
re-echo	renew
re-embark	reorganise
reinforce	repay
re-establish	replace
refill	reprint
refit	reproduction

More words beginning with RE—

reader	rectify
realize	rectory
reasonable	reduce

rebate..	reel..
recede......................................	refer ....
receipt	reference ....
recent......................................	refinery.....................................
recess	refuge..
recipe	refund ....
recite	regal...
recline	regent..
recollect..................................	regiment....................................
reconcile	registrar....................................
record......................................	regret ....
recruit	

Words beginning with STR—
Rule 43

straight...................................	stretcher....................................
straighten................................	strike ....
straightforward......................	strict..
stretch	

40

strain	stride
strand	strident
strange	strife
stranger	string
strangle	stringent
strap	strip
strategy	strive
stratum	stroke
straw	stroll
strawberry	strong
stream	stronger
strength	structure
strengthen	struggle
stress	

Words beginning with UNDER—

under	underscore
undercurrent	understand

undergo ....

understudy ....

underhand ....

undertook ....

undermine ....

underwent ....

underrate ....

underdone ....

undersize ....

underfoot ....

understood ....

undergrowth ....

undertone ....

underline ....

underwear ....

underpaid ....

undercut ....

undersigned ....

underestimate ....

understanding ....

underground ....

undertake ....

underlay ....

undervalue ....

underneath ....

underwrite ....

GENERAL DICTATION

The letters and articles given are based on a usual business vocabulary.

The chief feature of this section is that, when the common words are known, you should acquire the skill to write them faster and faster.

If a dictator is available, each letter or piece should be dictated twice; once within the writer's capacity and again at a higher rate.

Strive to reach increased speed the second time.

These exercises are intentionally of different lengths.

A student aspiring to speed may be able to sustain 100 words per minute for one minute when a piece of three minutes could be correctly taken down at only 90 words per minute. Exercises at bursts of speed and prolonged effort are both needed.

This section begins with exercises on the names of towns in Britain and in the rest of the world. Every writer should be able to write outlines for these names as instinctively as Brief Forms.

We must be able to take down in shorthand the names of towns and countries without a moment's hesitation. Let us begin with these:

BRITISH TOWNS AND CITIES

Aberdeen	*abdn*	Barrow	*bro*
Andover	*a—v*	Bath	*bt*
Ashford	*azfl*	Bedford	*bdfl*
Aylesbury	*alsby*	Bexhill	*bxl*
Banbury	*bnby*	Birkenhead	*brknhd*
Barnsley	*brnsl*	Birmingham	*br g*

43

Blackburn	bkbn	Buxton	bxtn
Bolton	bltn	Cambridge	k~bj
Bournemouth	brn~l	Canterbury	K-by
Bradford	bdf/	Cardiff	k/f
Brighton	btn	Carlisle	krll
Bristol	bsl	Chatham	ct~
Burnley	brnl	Chesterfield	cSfel
Bury	by	Colchester	klcS
		Coventry	kv-y

NOTE:

Names ending in	—bury	are given the ending	—by
,, ,,	—ham	,,	—m (omit H)
,, ,,	—bridge	,,	—bj
,, ,,	—ford	,,	—f/
,, ,,	—ly	,,	—l
,, ,,	—ton	,,	—tn
,, ,,	—worth	,,	—wrt

Crewe	ku	Dagenham	dgn~
Cromer	Ko	Darlington	drlgtn
Croydon	kydn	Derby	drb,

Devonport *dvnpl*	Edinburgh *ednbro*
Dewsbury *dzby*	Exeter *Xt*
Doncaster *dqs*	Falmouth *flt*
Dorchester *drcs*	Flint *f—*
Dorking *drk*	Folkestone *fksn*
Dover *Do*	Gateshead *gtsd*
Dundee *d—e*	Gillingham *flg*
Durham *dr*	Glasgow *gzgo*
Eastbourne *Ebrn*	Gloucester *gs*

Grantham *gnt*	Hammersmith *Hrst*
Great Yarmouth *q yrt*	Harwich *hrc*
Greenock *gnk*	Hastings *hsgs*
Grimsby *grsb;*	Hereford *hyfl*
Guildford *glfl*	High Wycombe *hu k*
Halifax *hlfx*	Holyhead *hlhd*

Huddersfield	*Hdsfel*	Lancaster	*lqs*
Inverness	*nv'*	Leeds	*lds*
Ipswich	*ypsc*	Leicester	*ls*
Jersey	*jrz,*	Lincoln	*lqn*
Kettering	*Kt*	Liverpool	*Lvpl*
Keighley	*ktl*	London	*l-n*
Kings Lynn	*kgsln*	Lowestoft	*losf*

Loughborough	*lfbro*	Middlesbrough	*dlsbro*
Luton	*lln*	Minehead	*nnhd*
Maidenhead	*dnhd*	Motherwell	*Ul*
Maidstone	*dsn*	Newcastle	*nksl*
Malvern	*lvn*	Newhaven	*nhvn*
Manchester	*mcs*	Newport	*np/*
Margate	*rga*	Northampton	*Nvpn*
Merthyr Tydfil	*Vr*	Norwich	*nrc*

46

Nottingham *nlg*

Oldham *old*

Oxford *xfl*

Paisley *pzl*

Pembroke *p bk*

Peterborough *Plbro*

Plymouth *prl*

Poole *pul*

Portsmouth *pll l*

Preston *psn*

Ramsgate *r sga*

Reading *rdg*

Reigate *rga*

Rochdale *rcdl*

Rochester *rcs*

Rotherham *Rl*

Rugby *rgb,*

Rye *ru*

St. Albans *s-albnz*

St. Helens *s-lnz*

Salford *slfl*

Sheffield *zfel*

Shrewsbury *zzby*

Slough *s*

Smethwick *s lk*

Southampton *s pn*

Southend *s-*

Southsea *sse*

South Shields *s zlds*

Southport		Sunderland	
Stockport		Swansea	
Stockton		Swindon	
Stoke		Taunton	
Stratford		Torquay	

Tilbury		West Hartlepool	
Tynemouth		Weymouth	
Wakefield		Wigan	
Wallasey		Wimbledon	
Walsall		Winchester	
Warrington		Windsor	
Warwick		Wolverhampton	
Watford		Worcester	
Wellington		Worthing	
West Bromwich		York	

48

Alexandria *alx-ra*

Amsterdam *sd*

Antwerp *a-rp*

Auckland *akl-*

Barcelona *brslna*

Belfast *blf,*

Belgrade *blgd*

Berlin *brln*

Bombay *b-ba*

Bonn *bn*

Brussels *bsls*

Buenos Aires *bnsrs*

Cairo *kro*

Calcutta *klkla*

Cape Town *kp hn*

Chicago *zkgo*

Colombo *kl-bo*

Copenhagen *kpnhgn*

Delhi *dl*

Detroit *Dyl*

Dublin *dbln*

Durban *drbn*

Hamburg *h-brg*

Helsinki *hlsq,*

Istanbul *isbl*

Johannesburg *jobrq*

Leningrad *lnngd*

Lisbon *lzbn*

Los Angeles *lsnylz*

Luxembourg *lx-brq*

Lyons *lins*

Madrid *dd*

49

City	Shorthand	City	Shorthand
Marseilles	*rsls*	Rio de Janeiro	*rio*
Melbourne	*lbn*	Rome	*ro*
Mexico City	*xko s)*	Rotterdam	*Rld*
Milan	*ln*	San Francisco	*fsko*
Montreal	*-rl*	Sao Paulo	*s plo*
Moscow	*sko*	Shanghai	*zghi*
New York	*ny*	Stockholm	*k*
Oslo	*ozlo*	Sydney	*sdn,*
Ottawa	*o a*	Tokyo	*tko*
Paris	*Ps*	Toronto	*tr-o*
Philadelphia	*fldlfa*	Vancouver	*vnkv*
Pekin	*pkn*	Vienna	*vna*
Prague	*pg*	Warsaw	*rsa*
Quebec	*qbk*	Wellington	*lgln*
		Washington	*zgln*

50

Algeria	*aljya*	England	*egl —*
Argentine	*aj-n*	Finland	*fnl —*
Australia	*aSla*	France	*f*
Austria	*aSa*	Germany	*jrmn,*
Belgium	*bly*	Ghana	*gna*
Brazil	*bzl*	Greece	*ges*
Britain	*bln*	Holland	*hl —*
Canada	*kda*	Hungary	*hgy*
Ceylon	*sln*	India	*nda*
Chile	*cl,*	Indonesia	*ndnza*
China	*cna*	Ireland	*rl —*
Congo	*kgo*	Israel	*izrl*
Czechoslovakia	*cko*	Italy	*ill*
Denmark	*dnrk*	Japan	*jpn*
Egypt	*eyp*	Jugoslavia	*ygslva*

51

Kenya	*kna*	Russia	*rɔza*
Malaya	*laa*	Scotland	*skll —*
Mexico	*xko*	South Africa	*Safka*
Netherlands	*Nel — —*	Spain	*sn*
New Zealand	*nuzl —*	Switzerland	*S zl —*
Nigeria	*nyya*	Sweden	*s dn*
Norway	*nr a*	Tanganyika	*lgnka*
Nyasaland	*nsl —*	Uganda	*ug — a*
Poland	*pl —*	United States	*usa*
Portugal	*p/gl*	Venezuela	*vnzla*
Rhodesia	*rdza*	Wales	*alz*

1

Dear Mr. Armstrong,

In these days of wise spending, we are inclined to practise 'economies' that really result in waste. /

There is a time in the life of every car when the cost of upkeep far exceeds the value of // the service that the car can render.　40
Today, new car prices are the lowest and new car values the greatest / in the history of the industry. Take advantage of this opportunity to trade in your old car for a // new one.　80

The Crescent showroom is near your home and open in the evenings for your convenience. Come and see / the new Crescent Eight and enjoy a demonstration ride. Our representative will be glad to explain our new easy-payment // plan.　120

Yours sincerely,　123

2.

Dear Sirs,

We expect to be able to send the booklets requested in your letter of October 10 some time during the / early part of next week.

We had hoped to have this unusual pamphlet, which is called *Planning the Ideal Kitchen*, // ready on October 1. Our printer,　40
who has been having production problems, told us yesterday that he will have a / small supply in our office on Saturday.

We are just as eager to see the finished book as you are //　80
because we know that the planning service in this publication is without doubt the best that has ever been offered / to home-owners.

Yours faithfully,　106

3.

Dear Sir,

We shall be pleased to send you our magazine free of charge for three months. We hope that / you will find it interesting, and helpful in your work. It includes all the latest news about trends and events // in the world of popular music, articles about show　40

53

business, and features about well-known people in the industry.

Read / the magazine at our expense for three months. At the
80 end of that time, we hope you will send us // an order for regular delivery.
87 Yours faithfully,

4.

Dear Mr. Barker,

I am sorry you have not been getting prompt supplies of our kitchenware from us lately. Your / last order came in at a time when we were already working overtime to clear a sudden spate
40 of orders // from customers.

However, we have increased our packing-room staff, and we shall be able to deal with your orders / more quickly in future.
66 Yours sincerely,

5.

Dear Sir,

I shall be taking my car on the Continent on August 24, returning on September 8. The Channel / crossing will be made in both directions by air (Air Flights Ltd.).
40 Particulars of the car are: Austin 10 saloon // HXT 683, engine number G4R4864X, chassis number GSI 260120.

The countries to be visited are: Belgium, Luxembourg, Western Germany, Switzerland / and France.

Am I right in assuming that my policy covers Continental
80 risks? Would you be kind enough to send // me a 'green card'— and information concerning insurance of personal luggage and against personal accident.
97 Yours faithfully,

6.

Dear Madam,

We have pleasure in inviting you, as one of our regular customers, to choose bargains at our Bradley / Street shop before the sale officially opens to the public on Thursday, January 7th.
40 We shall be pleased to see // you on any of the three days pre-

ceding that date, and we shall be glad to show you a full / range of dresses, twin-sets, coats, skirts, and hats, all at very greatly reduced prices.

We look forward to seeing // you and having the pleasure of serving you. 80

Yours faithfully, 90

7.

Dear Mr. Morgan,

I am a little worried because I have not yet received from you the manuscript for your / article on cloud formations for our September issue.

You will remember that you agreed to let me have this by // July 10, three days ago. If you remember, you let me have part of the article when you were in / the office a fortnight ago, but we are not able to have this set until we have the whole of // the material. 40

80

Please let me have the manuscript as soon as possible. If it is not on my desk within / the next two days, I shall have to hold it over for another issue.

Yours sincerely, 96

8.

Dear Mary,

I should like to offer as an autumn or February production "The Clouds" of Aristophanes.

There would be / 6 or 8 female parts (including either 4 or 6 in the Chorus). Two of these would be parts adapted // from roles written as male. 40

There would be 14 male parts, or 12 if two players double.

I should prefer / to use my own adaptation, in prose and blank verse. Failing this, there is one prose version which would do // at a pinch, and several verse translations which might also serve. 80

Yours sincerely. 93

9.

Dear Sir,

Again we must ask you to settle your account, the balance of

55

which is shown on the enclosed / statement. Although the sum not a large one, you must realize that we cannot wait so long
40 for a // cheque from you. The policy of our shop with credit customers is that all accounts must be paid in thirty / days.

Please write us a cheque now so that it is not again overlooked.
75   Yours faithfully,

10.

Dear Sir,

This is to remind you that your annual subscription to the Club is now due. May I draw / your attention to the increase in the subscription from five to six pounds per annum?
40   As explained when the increase // was approved at the recent annual general meeting, the Club is liable to incur heavy expenditure in the forthcoming year. / The library is being rebuilt, and to some extent restocked. It has been necessary to appoint
80   a permanent paid secretary // to cope with the increased correspondence. In addition the dining-room costs have risen sharply.

All this places a strain / on the Club's finances. You can help by kindly paying your subscription promptly, and this year we
120 are enclosing a // stamped addressed envelope in the hope that you will be able to do so.
136   Yours faithfully,

11.

Dear Sirs,

On September 3 I sent you an order for goods which should have been received by this time. / What is the reason for the delay? This is the first time in our experience that orders from
40   your company // have been so long in transit. We need these goods for a special purpose and if we do not receive / them in a few days, we shall be forced to cancel our order.
80   Usually you have been most prompt and // we are puzzled by this lapse.
88   Yours faithfully,

56

12

Dear Mr. Simpson,

Thank you very much for your recent letter asking us to send you the book on the / Peninsular war. From your description we are a little undecided, however, about which book you mean.

Do you mean the // book which you commented on when you last visited our shop, in July? Or do you mean the recent publication / which has had some favourable reviews in the Sunday press, in two volumes? 40

We can supply either book from stock, // but we should be glad to have your confirmation before we arrange to despatch it and invoice you. 80

Yours sincerely, 100

13.

Dear Sir,

With a view to increasing your paint sales we can print sales letters on your own stationery to / be sent to your customers. We should do the printing, fill in the addresses, address the envelopes and pay the // postage. 40

You will find that these letters will bring in good returns. We tried them last year for several dealers / with such good results that we now want you to have the benefit of this advertising plan.

We are enclosing // samples of the letters. Please read them over and then send us your list of names and addresses as soon / as possible, so that we can start this work for you. 80

Yours faithfully, 113

14.

Dear Miss Blue,

We are sending you our catalogue showing the material we carry for summer covers. This material is / available for immediate delivery. We also enclose our price list on which discount of ten per cent is offered for // cash. 40

If you do not find the type of material you wish, may we ask you to come to our / shop, where we have patterns from many houses in the city?

80   It is indeed a pleasure to be of service // to you.

84   Yours sincerely,

15.

Dear Reader,

I am sorry to remind you of the sad fact that your subscription to our magazine has quietly / expired.

However, there is still time to prevent the calamity of missing
40 the next number. It is always a disappointment // to miss an issue, for each one has a way of starting lively arguments and spirited talk, not to mention / the urge to independent thinking.

You have in your hands now a simple form that reduces to
80 a matter of // seconds the time required for renewing your subscription. Simply tear off this sheet, put it in an envelope. Slip your / cheque with the enclosed bill into it, too, and the
115 thing is done.

                              Yours sincerely,

16.

Dear Mrs. Locke,

We wonder why we have not received an order from you since last February. We have made / many changes in our departments since that time, and we wish you would give us the opportunity to serve you. //
40 We carry a new line of coats, dresses, and suits which I am sure will please you. The enclosed circular / will show you our new low prices for these goods. Perhaps you could arrange to
80 examine our stock when you / are in town.

85   Yours sincerely,

17.

Dear Sir,

Thank you very much for your cheque for £15.10.0. We have had no word from you since your / cheque was received. Was there anything wrong with our goods or our services?

If anything did not satisfy you in // our recent delivery, please   40
let us know. We want you to be pleased with everything we sell.

Yours faithfully,   59

18.

Dear Sirs,

The consignment of your blue ink received from you on
May 2 is below standard, according to complaints / received
from schools in the last few days.

We have distributed this under the Gladstone name for years
as a // washable blue ink, which can be removed from clothing   40
and furniture with soap and water. This ink is now particularly /
popular in elementary schools, where the washable feature is a
very strong selling point with the authorities concerned.

Reports from // schools that have used bottles from your   80
last delivery, however, indicate that something is wrong, and
we are deeply concerned. /

We are sending you a specimen from this lot and shall expect
a study of this matter and a prompt // report.   120

Yours faithfully,   122

19.

Dear Sirs,

Thank you for your order of May 26 for two dozen watches
amounting to £69.15.0. We shall try / to handle this order in a
way that will meet with your approval and be the means of
further extending // the business between us. A generous supply   40
of our advertising material will be sent with your order.

The rules of / all wholesale houses require that proper information be secured before they extend credit. This information
usually can be obtained from // references.   If you will send us   80
the name and address of your bank, we shall make the necessary
inquiries as / quickly as possible.

May we hear from you by return?

Yours faithfully,   112

59

20.

Dear Madam,

Did you find the new book we sent to you interesting reading? Would you like us to send / you additional books which we feel you would like? If you would like a book a month, please tick
40 where // it is indicated. Perhaps you would only like to receive reports of new books recently published and so decide for / yourself which would interest you.

Drop the card in the post so that we can be of service to
80 you. //
82   Yours sincerely,

21.

Dear Sir,

I am sorry to have to complain yet again about the finish of our new gas cooker.

You / will remember that you have already replaced the backplate, which was chipped at the time of installation, and that
40 you // have undertaken to replace the oven door and the grill pan because of flaking off of the enamel.

Now another / deficiency has become apparent.

The chromium-plated bars of the plate racks on either side of
80 the grill are rusting. // In one place the metal has rusted so badly that the chromium-plating is now missing over an area about / an inch and a half long, with spots beginning elsewhere. This has
120 happened although the chromium has been cleaned with // nothing more drastic than soap and water.

Would you please look into this new matter, also? No doubt in replacing / the other defective items, you will make sure that you replace the chromium-plated bars also.
160 This matter is becoming // a very considerable nuisance to me.

My complaint, like the others, is a reasonable and legitimate one, and I am / sure you will attend to it as promptly and cour-
200 teously as you did the others. It is a source of // some astonishment to me that so many defects can become apparent in the finish of a cooker in so short / a space of time.

226   Yours faithfully,

22

Dear Sir,

Kindly send me a cheque now for the balance due on your account. We do not like to / have to send letters like this to you, nor do we think that you like to receive them. However, in // order for us to do business, we have no choice in the matter but to make our position clear. I / am sure you have to do the same thing from time to time at your end.

We hope you will // give this letter immediate attention and that we shall find your payment in our office in a very short time. /

Yours faithfully,

40

80

102

23

Dear Madam,

In reply to your enquiry, we can supply a boy's sweater in a blue and tan combination for / 27/-.

Articles will be sent on approval to customers who have a credit account. We should be very glad to // number you among our credit customers if you would favour us with the required bank and business references on the / enclosed card.

If you prefer, you may send us an order with payment covering the cost. Should the goods not // be satisfactory on delivery, you may return any article not desired, provided this is done within a reasonable time, and / the goods are in saleable condition.

May we have the pleasure of serving you?

Yours faithfully,

40

80

116

24

My dear Miss Stewart,

Miss May Black has applied for a position with our firm and has given us your / name as a reference. We shall appreciate it if you will express your opinion regarding Miss Black, taking into consideration // her ability along general lines, the initiative that she has shown in her school work, and her inclination to

40

assume / responsibility. When writing your letter, please con-
80 sider also her character and her health // and give us any other
relevant details.

We shall treat confidentially any facts that you may care to
give us. If your letter is addressed to Box 20, / it will be delivered
to me personally, in my private office.
120 We assure you that you co-operation in this matter // will be
appreciated.
125 Yours sincerely,

25.

Dear Sir,

Thank you for your letter of April 5th.

I am delighted that you are willing to display our / posters in
your licensed houses in the Burlesden area, before and during
our summer production.
40 We very much appreciate your // co-operation over this, and
also your generosity in saying that you would rather pay for the
advertising in our programme. /

I am able to offer you a half page across in this programme
80 at 50 shillings, and I enclose a // copy of last year's programme.
As you see, a half page across has a type area of 4 inches across /
by 3½ down. Copy should be in the hands of our Business Mana-
120 ger, Mr. Robert Lucas, 139 Sheen Park, on // or before May 15.
The show will be given this year from July 9 to July 14 inclusive.

Perhaps you / would be kind enough to confirm that you
160 wish to take the space offered, and also to let me know // how
many posters you will require and to whom they should be
delivered.

We shall be printing two sizes of / poster—Double Crown
(20 x 30) and Demy Folio (11¼ x 17½).

With many thanks for your help.
200 Yours faithfully, //

26.

The first head I ever tried to paint was an old woman with
the upper part of the face shaded / by her bonnet, and I certainly
laboured at it with great perseverance. It took me numberless

62

sittings to do it. // I have it by me still, and sometimes look at 40
it with surprise, to think how much pains were thrown / away
to little purpose; yet not altogether in vain if it taught me to see
good in everything, and to // know that there is nothing vulgar 80
in Nature seen with the eye of science or of true art. Refine-
ment creates / beauty everywhere; it is the grossness of the
spectator that discovers nothing but grossness in the object.
Be this as // it may, I spared no pains to do my best. If art was 120
long, I thought that life was so / too at that moment. 144

(From William Hazlitt's 'Essay on the Pleasures of Painting')

27.

Joe lay awake till the moon was up and the rest were asleep.
Then he took his gun and went / out to do what he had to do.
By night-time his crime would seem less. Dizzy and unsteady
on // his feet, he staggered away from the wagon. He found 40
'Missouri', and the half-tame doe started away from him / as if
knowing his purpose.

He followed as she moved towards a little natural fortress of
rocks and boulders.

The // doe stopped and turned her head. Joe raised the gun 80
to his shoulder. The target seemed to swim before his / eyes and
he pulled the trigger.

There was a sort of scream. Joe stumbled forward to the
rocks. Among them // he found the dead body of a buck. An old, 120
ugly buck that would taste as tough as buffalo. He / felt it and
it was still warm. There was a bullet hole in its head. 155

(From 'Amy and the Doe' by John Holmes, Aberdeen Press
and Journal, 1960)

28.

String is my foible. My pockets get full of little hanks of it,
picked up and twisted together, ready for / uses that never come.
I am seriously annoyed if any one cuts the string of a parcel
instead of patiently // and faithfully undoing it fold by fold. 40
How people can bring themselves to use indiarubber rings,
which are a / sort of deification of string, as lightly as they do,
I cannot imagine. To me an indiarubber ring is // a precious 80

treasure. I have one which is not new—one that I picked up off the floor nearly six / years ago. I have really tried to use it, but my heart failed me, and I could not commit the // extrava-
121 gance.

(From 'Cranford' by Mrs. Gaskell)

29.

Dear Mr. Robinson,

It was very good of you to send me the testimonial I asked you for, and you / have been most generous in your praises.

Unfortunately, I have to ask you to be kind enough to send
40 me // a carbon copy, because the top copy is now unusable.

I worked later than usual at the office yesterday and / was the last to leave. I took down to the front door a milk bottle which
80 the tea girl had // evidently forgotten, meaning to leave it by the front door.

Half an hour later I found myself standing in the / train, clutching my brief case in one hand and an empty milk bottle
120 in the other. I felt distinctly foolish. //

In my embarrassment, I stuffed the bottle into my brief case. Unfortunately the bottle could not have been quite clean, / because when I got home I found that it had leaked over my papers and had spoilt the testimonial.
160   Would // you be kind enough to send a carbon?
170   Yours sincerely,

30.

Dear Mr. Robinson,

How very kind of you to send me the carbon copy of the testimonial, especially as it / is the only copy you have.

I regret to say this copy is now useless also.
40   While waiting on the // station platform to go to the office yesterday, I was surprised to see a man lying on his tummy between / the tracks.

Very foolishly I jumped down on the line to help him to his
80 feet. He began to swear // at me, which made me angry, and would not be persuaded back on the platform.

64

I began to shout at / him and tried to pull him away. He then menaced me with a heavy spanner, and I realised that // he was 120 in fact a railway employee who had been tightening the nuts holding the fishplates in place.

People on / the platform suddenly began to scream and shout, and we realised that a train was approaching the platform.

We scrambled // clear just in time, but unfortunately I left 160 my brief-case behind, and this was sliced neatly in two by / the wheels, leaving all my papers—and the testimonial—soaked in oil.

Would it be too much trouble to ask // you to send me a new 200 testimonial? In view of my carelessness, perhaps you will want to make certain omissions / from your remarks this time! 225

31.

Dear Mr. Clark,

Of course it is not too much trouble to provide a new testimonial. I have much pleasure / in enclosing it.

Far from omitting anything, I have actually added to it, as you see, to say that I // have never had the pleasure of knowing 40 a more charming, more plausible, nor more insensitive idiot in my life, nor / one whose engaging personality would make him less fitted to a position of responsibility.

If these additions do not seem // sufficient, I should of course 80 be happy to oblige by enlarging further.

Yours sincerely, 94

32.

Dear Sirs,

Knowing that you employ a large number of book-keepers and office assistants in your establishment, I respectfully / apply for a position as book-keeper.

I am twenty-two years old, was brought up on a farm, and with // the exception of the past two years have always lived in 40 the country. Two years ago I passed through my / local business college and I secured advanced level in the R.S.A. examination last year. For six months I was with // the Produce Exchange 80 Bank. During the past year I have worked for the Guardian

65

Trust Company, 170 Broadway. I left / the Produce Exchange Bank to better myself with the Guardian Trust Company. As
120 there seemed to be very little opportunity // in the banking business I terminated my connection with the Guardian Trust Company on March 1st of this year. I am enclosing their reference.

I am strong, healthy and unmarried. My training has been
160 such as to fit me // especially to initiate any ordinary set of books and keep them according to the most approved modern methods. I realise / that I am a young man, and I am very
200 desirous to succeed. Wherever I am employed I expect to // earn my money; and I am willing to work hard and put in long hours. My employer's interest shall always / be mine and I shall do all I can to please.

240 I have no bad habits, keep regular hours, and // try to be pleasant and obliging to all. While I am especially fitted for a book-keeper's position, I feel / that I could enter fully into the pattern of your organisation in any way required.

280 Should you be able to // use such a man in any capacity, I shall be glad to begin with you at a salary of £20 / a week.

I hope to hear that you have a vacancy for me.

315   Yours sincerely,

                            33.

Western Hardware Corporation,
3 Broad Street,
Bristol 7.

Dear Sirs,

In a few days you will receive our new catalogue of hand tools.

The purpose of this catalogue / is to provide our dealers with a complete list of hand tools and supplies for which there is a
40 steady // demand. The clear explanations and descriptions will make it easy for you to make your selections.

From experience you know / that Medlock tools are designed and built for skilled workmen. For more than sixty years our
80 firm has been a // recognized source of supply for dependable tools.

We advise you to look through your requirements now while our stock is complete, / because no one knows what the demand will be in a few months.

Yours faithfully,

115

34.

Western Hardware Corporation,
3 Broad Street,
Bristol 7.

Dear Sirs,

We are writing to urge that you permit us to fulfil your hand tool order while we are / in a position to do so.

Since we sent you our new catalogue in August, the demands upon the manufacturers // of hand tools have greatly increased. 40
We have increased the production capacity of our factory in an effort to co-operate / fully with our customers in their increasing needs. We are doing our best to supply our dealers all over the // country with the same high-quality hand tools that 80
have made the name of Medlock famous and much sought after.

We can assure you that there will be no price changes before November 1. Your order can be // handled promptly now. 120
Yours faithfully, 125

35.

Western Hardware Corporation,
3 Broad Street,
Bristol 7.

Dear Sirs,

Thank you for your letter of October 10, in which you enclosed two purchase orders. We do appreciate / this business and are glad that you have given us the chance to supply some of your further needs // before any adjustments in prices are 40
necessary.

Prices may rise in November.

The manager of our despatch department has received / orders to speed up the Molton Technical School order. You may feel

67

80 certain that this equipment will reach the school // without delay. We are just as eager as you are to maintain your reputation for superior service with speed, courtesy, / and efficiency.

The rapid growth of industrial courses in large cities during **120** the past few years means increased tool business. // Here is a good opportunity to increase your sales and be of real service in a bigger way.

140   Yours faithfully, //

36.

Western Hardware Corporation,
3 Broad Street,
Bristol 7.

Dear Sirs,

This morning we received a request to submit a bid on the equipment that will be needed for / the new technical school now being erected in Taunton and due for completion in August.

40   It is our policy, as // you know, to work only through our regular dealers. Therefore, we suggest that you send a representative to follow up / this opportunity for some very good business.

We can be very helpful to you in preparing your estimate on **80** the // list of hand tools, and we hope you will let us work with you. The large machine equipment, / of course, is out of our line. Because of your long experience in this field, we know you **120** will have // no trouble in submitting a complete list.

129   Yours faithfully,

37.

Shaw and Spooner,
89 John Street,
Nottingham.

Dear Sirs,

Our records show that just one year ago today your first order reached our office. We are happy / to express our appreciation of your orders.

68

This year of pleasant and profitable business friendship we hope will be // one of many.   40

We realize, of course, that the goodwill of our old friends and the confidence of our new customers / depend directly on our goods and the quality of our service. Therefore, we are eager to have your frank opinion. // Will you please use the   80 enclosed questionnaire and addressed envelope to let us know how we may be of service / to you?   100

Yours faithfully,   104

38.

William Shaw, Esq.,
Shaw and Spooner,
89 John Street,
Nottingham.

Dear Mr. Shaw,

Thank you for the prompt attention given to our questionnaire. We also appreciate your letter of April 8 / because it gives us an opportunity to study your problem. We want you to feel that this company is // always interested in the success of your   40 business and new projects in every possible way.

We have, therefore, directed Mr. / James King of our credit department to discuss terms of payment with you.

Mr. King will get in touch with // you about this when he   80 is in your town on other business. If it is convenient for you, he can / discuss your problem with you either before or after another appointment he has at noon on February 15.

Mr. King // will telephone you next week to see if this suits   120 you.

Yours sincerely,   133

39.

William Shaw, Esq.,
Shaw and Spooner,
89 John Street,
Nottingham.

Dear Mr. Shaw,

Thank you for your courtesy to Mr. King, who reports that he had a very satisfactory discussion / with you on February 15.

69

Mr. King believes that he understands your problem and that
40 you realize how important it // is for us to maintain a uniform credit policy.

Whenever it seems necessary, as Mr. King pointed out to you, / we shall be glad to consider a request for an extension of
80 the discount period to enable you to meet // an unusual situation.

Mr. King was favourably impressed by your modern shop with its complete stock. Our high-quality products, / of course, belong in your type of shop. We assure you, therefore, of our
120 sincere desire to co-operate with you. //
122   Yours sincerely,

40.

William Shaw, Esq.,
Shaw and Spooner,
89 John Street,
Nottingham.

Dear Mr. Shaw,

We are glad that you did not hesitate to write to us concerning the credit problems in / connection with your autumn order for sporting and other goods.
40   Because of your excellent credit rating and the volume of //
business which you have given us, we shall be happy to accept your order and date the invoice September 1. / This arrangement will extend the discount period to October 10.
80   It is sound business to save by taking advantage of // discounts. We realize how you feel because we make every effort to plan our collections so that we also may / discount our invoices. We are able, as a result, to offer our high-quality products at very attractive prices.
121   Yours // sincerely,

41.

Dear Sir,

I am writing a short article for the local paper on Belstone Castle, in view of the fifth / centenary of the raising of the siege

by the Duke of Parlby, which falls next month. I enclose a
rough // draft of the article.   40

I am looking for suitable photographs to illustrate the article,
and do not wish to choose / those which will already be well
known to readers of the paper through familiarity with the
official series of picture // postcards. I wonder whether you are   80
able to help me by showing suitable prints? A picture of the
west gateway / would be useful, in view of the important role
this played during the siege, and I should also like to // include   120
a picture of the interior of the dining hall.

Perhaps you would be good enough to show me some //
material?

Yours faithfully,   143

42.

Dear Mr. Matthews,

Thank you for your enquiry for a fifty-ton twisting machine for installation in your works. From / what you tell me
about your requirements, I should think that the model we
call RD 25 is the one // most likely to suit you.   40

Bampton and Clarke, of Bundlesham, have one of these
machines, which we installed for them / some seven years ago,
and I could make arrangements for you to inspect their machine
and see it in operation. //   80

The first requirement, however, is for our representative,
Mr. Brinklow, to call on you and talk about your particular
needs. / I shall ask Mr. Savage, our Chief Engineer, to go with
him to meet any of your staff for a // discussion of the project.   120

It should certainly be possible to produce and install the
machine by September, as you stipulate, / provided the speci-
fication can be completed in detail by the end of May. The only
major complication will be the // modification to our standard   160
design to fit the rather limited distance between the retaining
walls which you mentioned. This will / involve considerable
work at the drawing board.

Yours faithfully,   189

43.
A NOSE FOR TROUBLE

Catarrh is perhaps the commonest, and at the same time most misunderstood, affliction there is in / this country. The medical dictionaries agree that it is an inflammation of a
40 mucous membrane, and go on to list // eighteen different kinds of catarrh, according to which membrane is involved.

Three obvious examples are bronchial catarrh, catarrh of the / stomach, and catarrh of the bladder. But most people apply
80 the word in only one sense, meaning chronic rhinitis. And // this inflammation of the mucous membrane lining of the nose
102 is what most people mean when they say the have / got catarrh.

(From The Sunday Times, 3/12/61)

44.

Dear Mr. Hartley,

I am most grateful to you for giving me the opportunity of considering the enclosed manuscript for / a book on pathology. This is certainly a most interesting and expert work, but I
40 regret we should not be // interested in publishing it.

It is true we published the three-volume work by Chatley eight years ago, and this / is a standard work of reference, but it has ceased to be our policy to produce medical and scientific
80 works, // and we are now concentrating almost entirely on works of natural history and geography—subjects in which we have built / up a considerable reputation.

May I suggest that you should show your work to my friend,
120 Mr. Arthur Jones of // the Waters and Wainwright Press? They are tending to become specialists in the particular line of country which you cover./
142   Yours sincerely,

45.

The Circulation Manager,
Woodis and Gunn Ltd.

Dear Sir,

You may not believe this, but it is true.

Last August / or September I ordered a regular monthly

supply, via my newsagent, of Red Carnation Romances. I have
not received a copy of // this book from that day to this.   40
I wrote to you on March 2 to protest over the delay. You /
sent me back a courteous letter promising action in the matter,
and I looked forward to some results. There have // been none.   80
I should have thought it would be a very simple thing to buy
these books. It seems instead / to be the most difficult thing in
the world. Something is very wrong somewhere along the line
of distribution, and // if many customers have had experiences   120
like mine, you must be losing a lot of revenue.
May I take it / that you will see these books are supplied now
and every month to my newsagent?

Yours faithfully.   157

46

SAVING

Wealth that we have created is available for our enjoyment,
but it need not be used immediately. If we like. / we may save
the wealth for use at another time. Some forms of wealth can
be saved directly by storing; // but some forms are either   40
perishable or bulky, and these cannot be saved. They must be
exchanged for some other / form of wealth convertible into
consumable products.

Thus one saves primarily by saving money. This process is
necessary to the // individual in our society, as it is the only way   80
in which he can assure himself of a continued living / when he
ceases producing as the result of age, illness, or accident, or
when he wishes to retire or to // take a holiday; and it is the only   120
way in which he can procure luxuries which cost more than
his / current earnings.

Savings take many forms. Besides the direct hoarding of cash
or of imperishable consumer goods, saving may occur // through   160
the lending of money and the building up of a credit. This takes
the form of bank deposits, or / interest-bearing deposits in a
savings-bank, or interest-bearing loans to individuals or companies by notes, mortgages, or bonds. // In addition, it is   200

possible to save by buying interests which are less directly convertible into money, such as property, / buildings, shares in business ventures, and common stocks of public companies.
240 The attraction of any form of saving lies in // the possibility of converting the savings into consumer goods, and this is possible because at any time there are other / individuals who are willing to accept the saved wealth in exchange for the consumer goods
280 which are constantly being produced. // The value of savings, then, depends upon the continuance of our form of society; but within that form its importance / to the individual is prac-
307 tically beyond calculation.

47.
MARKET PRICE

When a given commodity changes hands with reasonable frequency, a certain competition is instituted between buyers to find sellers, and / between sellers to find buyers. The result is a reduction of the price demanded by the seller and an in-
40 crease // in the price offered by the buyers until agreement is reached on a compromise or fair price. Thus the price / of any article commonly bought and sold is in a sort of equilibrium
80 between two forces, the forces of supply // and the forces of demand.

If this equilibrium is in any way disturbed, the nature of the situation immediately produces / a new equilibrium. If the supply of an article is increased, or the demand lessened, some
120 sellers will be unable // to find buyers and will in consequence reduce their prices. As the price falls, fewer sellers are willing to sell / and more buyers are willing to buy, until the fall in price
160 produces a new equalization of buying and selling, // or of supply and demand, at a new price level lower than that which was previously obtained. If the supply / of any article is de-creased, or the demand increased, some buyers are unable to
200 find sellers, and so increase their // bids until the higher bids attract new sellers and repel some of the old buyers to a suffi-
224 cient extent to / establish a new equilibrium.

48
ABILITY TO WORK WITH OTHERS

Someone has suggested that the chief reason for individual failure in occupations is lack of ability to work well with / others. This, far more than any lack of competence and skill, accounts for dismissal, with the consequent dislocation and unhappiness. // This is the common experience of those who have   40
responsibility for handling personnel at all levels of employment. While that / fact is generally recognized, it has not been adequately reflected in educational emphasis. Knowledge, skill in writing and speaking, training // for vocations, have been   80
considered the chief objectives of the educational process. Relatively little attention has been given to developing / the attitudes and outlook necessary to effective co-operation with others.

The tragedy and waste evident in the career of the // mal-   120
adjusted individual are multiplied a thousandfold when transferred to the group. Labour-management disputes which result in strikes and lockouts // are at bottom simply failures in human   160
relations. The interests of both groups are basically the same. Both depend upon / the success of the enterprise in which they are engaged, and neither can succeed without the other; yet the waste // caused by industrial conflicts is incalculable.   200

The story of a recent strike and its settlement early in this year through a change in attitude on the part of the chairman of the company and a trade union leader is a // clear demonstra-   240
tion of the fact that the most aggravated dispute can be settled quickly once the contending parties look at / the real issue. Apparently the settlement resulted from both parties deciding to try to answer the question '*what* is right' // instead of talking   280
about '*who* is right'.

In a highly industrialized and complex society, a strike in one industry, as / all of us know, results in enforced idleness not only of the // employees of that industry but of others which   320
depend upon products of the striking company. The result is that a major waste in manpower resources in recent years / has resulted from these conflicts. The schools, by emphasizing the crucial importance of skill in human relations, could have an //   360

appreciable effect, in the long run, on domestic conflicts of all kinds; they would thereby add materially to the effective / man-
385 power resources of the country.

49.

CREATING A CLIMATE OF CONFIDENCE

Public confidence is the one element without which men cannot hope to build a thriving, prosperous, and continuing business. The / task of winning the public's trust in the integrity of business enterprises starts, of course, with the individual
40 company or // organization. But in this highly competitive world, the effort of a single man or company to maintain public confidence and / a climate where business can be conducted fairly, honestly and profitably is not enough.
80 The public, when faced with unfair // business tactics, does not always dispose of the situation with: 'I should have known better. I'll never go near that / place again.'

Instead, the entire business or industry is often judged by
120 the actions of a few individuals. Confidence is // easily under-mined, and the responsible organizations as well as the irre-sponsible feel the loss of income and decrease of profits. / In the same manner, a few false announcements can destroy trust
160 and belief in advertising whether in newspapers or on // tele-vision.

To offset this and to prevent the harm which can be caused by the errors of even a single / firm it is necessary to employ collective action—action in which every businessman and
198 organization has a vital stake.

50.

YOU AND YOUR PERSONALITY

All of us hear so much spoken about our personality. We have some idea of what is meant by the / word, yet few of us would try to give an exact definition of it. We all know that a
40 person // is known by his personality, and of course we all want

76

to have a good, pleasing personality. Everyone wants to / be highly thought of by friends and by all with whom he comes in contact.

You might roughly divide personality // into two parts; the 80 outward one which we call our appearance, and the inner one which we may call character. / Strangers may judge you entirely by appearance.

When you come into an office for the first time, you are quickly // sized up by the person who is interviewing you. He 120 looks at you and almost unconsciously he forms an opinion. / Of course it is your hope that this first impression is a good one. Whether it is a good one or not // may depend upon whether 160 you have the same idea as the interviewer of what an attractive appearance is. The first / thing he looks for is a neat, tidy, polite and genial impression. In dressing for your interview, remember you are // going to an office, not to a party, and choose your 200 clothes accordingly. This generally means simple attire with coat, / dress or suit, hat, shoes, gloves, all to match. Your hair, of course, should be neatly set.

The 'way you // walk can make a strong impression on a 240 person whose job is to interview people. Is your step firm? Does / it show quiet, easy self-confidence? Do you hold your head up, your chin up, your shoulders back? Are you // relaxed, 280 and do you have a smile on your face? Is there a minimum of make-up and yet sufficient / to show the good lines of your face? Are the seams of your stockings straight at the back? Or 320 do // you feel that you are perhaps presenting a false exterior?

All this an experienced personnel manager takes it at one / glance. If the firm you are calling upon is a good one, if it is a place where you are // anxious to work, then remember that the 360 personnel manager is very careful to select only those people who will fit into /this organization. When he talks to you, don't interrupt him. Let him finish each statement or question and then answer. //   400

Keep the following in mind if you wish to make a good first impression. Make the interviewer *want* you to / work in his organization. Then unconsciously, he wants to help you secure the position that you seek. You have won // the greater part 440

77

of the interview with a good impression. Your good personality has carried over to your interviewer so / that he becomes your friend and helper.

51.
YOUR LETTERS MUST BE BEAUTIFUL

Your letters are your company's ambassadors of good will, and just as you may judge a business firm by a / representative who calls upon you, so other firms will judge your firm by the
40 letters you write. Many executives // remark that they consider the quality of a secretary's transcript a major factor in evaluating her services. Over and over / again, men have said: 'Please include in your booklet a few hints telling secretaries and short-
80 hand typists how they can // make their letters beautiful'.

Here are some points to watch. See that the letter is properly centred. Make sure that / the margins are as even as possible.
120 Learn to use the tabulator for statistical and other work. If you are // using a manual typewriter, develop an even touch. You should always be able to produce a uniform density of appearance, / and still type with both speed and accuracy.

Your letters are a reflection of your personality, so never
160 release a // letter until you have checked it and can say to yourself: 'This is a job well done.'

Even/though filing may not be one of your duties, you should
200 know its fundamentals. You are a better secretary if // you can promptly produce correspondence that your boss needs. It is always very irritating to have to keep an / important long-distance caller waiting while the secretary searches for a letter,
240 or to be told blankly that 'the // file cannot be found anywhere.'

The executive likes to be quite sure that you and the dictionary agree on spelling. An / incorrectly spelled or an improperly divided word is a reflection on you, your employer,
280 and your whole organization. It is // an inexcusable mistake. To guard against such errors, you keep a dictionary handy always. Check any time there is a / shade of doubt, and never guess at unfamiliar terms.
320 Check, too, for all other errors before you submit a letter //
322 for signature.

52.

TRAVEL AND HOLIDAYS

My comments, last Autumn, on the functions of travel agents caused numbers of readers to say, can we tell which / agents are reliable?

A personal recommendation is, of course, the best evidence as to the competence of an agent. If // your friends the Blanks   40 have for many years let Messrs. X make all their travel arrangements, which have been carried / out to their complete satisfaction, it is highly unlikely that if you too put your trust in Messrs. X, you // will be let down. The same thing applies to the large,   80 old-established agents who have, over the years, prospered / greatly; such businesses are not built on inefficiency and sharp practice.

The real difficulty, however, arises when an advertisement for // a tour that attracts very much is published by a travel 120 agent who is completely unknown. And, I would repeat, / it is far from easy for the layman to judge whether or not the agent concerned is reputable and efficient. //   160

There are, however, some signposts; advertising material is the most useful of these. The rogues of the trade set out / to attract by price, impressive name, and extravagant claims.

It is well to remember that the very large agents operating // 200 in the main market can offer highly competitive prices, and it is very unlikely indeed that they can be / substantially undercut by a small, recently established agent.

Shop around, in the travel business, and see what sort of prices // the large, famous agents are quoting for the type of 240 tour that you have in mind. If you discover that / they are asking substantially more than are smaller agencies for what would appear to be much the same thing, you // can be pretty sure 280 that something is wrong somewhere. In such circumstances, it is a safe bet that it is / the small, unknown agent who is not going to live up to his promises.

Another good check, if this // is at all feasible, is to call— 320 or if you cannot do it, get a friend to call—in person / at the office of the agent.

If a personal call is impossible, remember that details of
360 registered companies can be // obtained from Bush House,
London. Knowledge of the date when the travel agent in question began trading, its directors, and / capital, can be useful,
too.

I would not wish to imply that all new, small, modestly-
400 officed travel agents are // crooked; but it is my experience that
such agents, if they are in fact competent and honest, do / not
resent frank inquiries as to their standing. Such firms realise
440 that they have yet to build up a good // reputation and, being
anxious to do this, they are very willing to give references.

Booking conditions are also a / fruitful source of information
as to the integrity of the agent; this is a complicated subject
480 about which it is // my intention to write later.

(From The Sunday Times, 13.5.1962)

53.

To enter the business world is really exciting.

Some may disagree. According to their point of view and
circumstances, some / feel driven to it to make a living or are
thrown into commercial life by hereditary and family ties.
40 Nevertheless, // allowing for exceptions, business provides
interests and rewards not found in other occupations. A few
words of advice are needed / at the start.

First, do not go into an occupation unless you think you will
80 like it. Vacancies are very // varied and numerous, but the
choice is yours. Provided you can make your choice after training in secretarial skills why / should you work for an engineer
if you like medical subjects? Why work in a bank if you like
120 the // stage? If travel appeals to you, apply to travel agencies.
If you have languages at your command try for a / post with
an exporter.

You really need to decide for yourself what you can take up
160 with enthusiasm. That is // the first requisite of entry into
business.

The second piece of advice is perhaps obvious. Do you like
working with / other people or do you prefer working alone?

If you like contact with many people, aim for the big firms. //
If you would like to work on your own, a personal secretary's 200
post is ideal. One thing to remember is / that competition in a
big firm is keener and promotion slower. Your training needs
to be of a high standard // to enter; but often large firms suit 240
young people.

There are other factors which may make an otherwise charming post / hateful. Travel is the first. A good opening that means
an hour or so on trains or buses should not // be entertained. 280
It looks all right at an interview, but travel when you are tired
at night can be most depressing. / Salary is the next factor. In
your reckoning you must take off travelling expenses, income
tax, pension subscriptions and all // regular outgoings, and then
see if the job is worth while to you.

Promotion prospects are another item to consider. / If you are
keen to get into a big firm whose reputation you admire you
may secure a foothold with // a low salary and promise of rises. 360
But you should make quite clear that you intend to progress,
and most / employers welcome this. It shows them from the out-
set that you intend to do your best.

Working conditions, hours of // work, and holidays all enter 400
into the good and bad points of a post. These being settled to
your satisfaction, / you can work happily and business will be
exciting.

54.

Here are a few hints on comportment in your post.

Posts are very different from one another, and I do / not
know what kind of post you are going to get. But *any* post is
very different from school or // from any other circle in which 40
you may have been.

Work is much harder if you do not like your / post. Many
personnel managers selecting to fill a post do not take anyone
who is not likely to enjoy her // work. If you enjoy your work 80
you do it well, and the reverse is true. So do not take a / post
unless you can find interest in it and do the work down to the
smallest detail, for all you // are worth. 120

Make friends of those you work with; it makes work easier. Be helpful to superiors and inferiors alike. / As you get on, there will be new people coming in below you, and everything

160 will be strange to them, // as it was to you at first. You are in a position to explain and show them the easiest and / best ways of doing things. You will make helpful fellow workers by this and

200 you may want to ask them // favours later on; they will be ready to help you because of their gratitude.

Punctuality is a delicate subject—I / am going to face it here. Some work late and early, others work early and late; the

240 former are noted // with reserve, the latter with approval— though nothing may be said. Only the latter get rises in salaries.

You are / never on your top form for 15 minutes after you

280 start, so try to get to your desk 15 minutes // before time. Steady yourself, get stationery and supplies for the day so that you are not held up in the / rush. At the other end of the day,

320 finish the job you are on. Do not watch the clock. Go // home with the feeling that you have finished the day, not done the minimum for your pay.

An exemplary attitude / in manner and appearance pays handsomely. Dress tidily but not showily.

360 Make-up should help nature, but should not look // artificial. Ban excessive jewellery and startling colours. Hair should be neat and glossy, not elaborate—something that looks as cared- / for at the end of the day as at the beginning. All this need not be costly.

400 Do not advertise // yourself. An egotistical attitude in speech or comportment is contemptible. To talk of your good points implies they are not / evident, and lets you down badly.

Do not have preferences. If you have preferences among the

440 staff or customers, it // means you have dislikes also. Treat all alike in business, irrespective of what you do outside. You may be married / to the boss's son, or hope to be, but that gives you

480 no prestige in office hours. Keep steady no // matter how people treat you. Whether they dislike you or are charmed with you, treat them all alike in business / hours. You will be in difficulties if five or six are enamoured with your charms! Outside the

529 office you can // let yourself go, but inside you must keep steady.

55.

'I hate typewriting—the noise—doing it over and over again —going quicker and quicker. I don't want to spend / my life pounding a typewriter'.

So said a student in one of our first-class commercial schools. Her companion added : // 'I feel the same way; Miss Frost says 40 it's a phase. Phase or not, it's a sheer waste of time. / Shorthand I don't mind. There is something to learn and think about. But typewriting! I could find something much more // useful to 80 do. . . .

'Come to think of it, shorthand and typewriting go together. What is the use of one without / the other ? Some people hate shorthand, some typewriting, so you can't do much about it anyway. I have read somewhere // that both skills become habits and 120 when they are habits you don't have to think about them, so you soon / will not think about your beloved shorthand. Then that won't be. interesting any longer. I suppose when they are both // habits and as thoughtless as walking, you won't bother 150 about either'.

This philosophy was a bit unanswerable; Florence pondered it. / She did really want to get on, to work for somebody nice, in work she found interesting. But the way // to that job was 200 what she had not bargained for. It was nice to dream of a post that was / all it ought to be and nothing it ought not to be; the job was to be for her interest // and gain, the salary was to be 240 large, the conditions were to suit her, the boss was to be ideal. / To her the school seemed a nuisance unnecessary to her life. She thought she could well do without it, and // would do the 280 minimum of work and minimum of home-work. The course was to be completed with the least inconvenience / to her.

Florence was, though she would not admit it, a shirker. Of course the inference was that in her // dream-post, she would 320 do only the work she liked and only the amount of it she liked.

In her / opinion, the class was full of people who did a lot of work which she did not intend to bother // with. The teacher's 360 efforts seemed outside her life. She counted the weeks when the course would be over. She was / always very low down in class,

83

and she hated the tests that came from time to time. What did
400 they // matter? She was no better off if she was higher up.

She had no ambition for the laurels of success. / What did it
matter if she was first or twenty-first?
440 There was a lecture one day that impressed // Florence
greatly. Afterwards she could not remember it all, but one thing
lurked in her mind, and constantly came back to / her with
recurring emphasis. It was this, 'no one is ever paid for what
480 they do, but for knowing how // to do it! The lecturer said
something like that, and it seemed an astonishing thing to say.
Pay had not / interested her much till then, but she thought
520 good pay would be an advantage, and good pay was given for //
'knowing how to do it'. It did not take any complicated reason-
ing to see that that was what she was / at school for. She had to
learn how to do the right things. She might do a lot that was //
quite useless to her employer. This would in the end be quite
useless to her, too.

With these thoughts, Florence / decided to devote more
attention to her studies, to acquire skill in doing things the best
way.
600 It was well-nigh // too late, to make up for lost time, and it
was a staggering blow to Florence to have to wake / up to the
reality of the economics that govern employer and employee.
640 She determined she would really learn the best // way to do what
she was going to be paid to do. Her one regret was that she had
not / realised this cardinal need earlier. Henceforth, she would
devote herself to both typewriting and shorthand. The best way
685 of doing // both was vital to her.

56.

DEFENCE AGAINST BURNING

Most responsible families are careful about guarding against
burns and scalds. But every year there are 700 deaths due to /
burns and scalds and some 50,000 people are so badly burnt
that they need hospital treatment.
40 The first line of // defence is that all fires, coal, gas or electric,
should have effective and secure guards.

84

The second, for babies and / toddlers especially, is easy. Get them into pyjamas rather than nightdresses as soon as you can. And insist on flame // -proof material.　　　　　　　　　　　80

Thirdly, you need knowledge about what to do if an accident happens. If clothing does catch fire, smother / the flames in a blanket, a rug, a coat, any heavy material you can seize, anything that will exclude air. // It is movement that creates　120 draughts and fans the flames.　　　　　　　　　　　130

(From The Sunday Times, 17.9.1961)

57.

If Poetry can survive fifty years of mass education it can survive anything. It has been misrepresented and deliberately mislaid; / its anaemic double discovered on calendars and coo'd over by maiden ladies with cups of tea. Patience Strong and Matriculation // Boards have done their worst; but it is still　40 published. If it sells badly, then it always sold badly—to / start with; and quite recently we've started with several poets who are now selling well. If bogus verse had its // big success in the last　80 century (just as some of the poetry of that age which now sells well had / its incredible failures), so it has had amazing sales in the last ten years.　　　　　　　　　　　114

(From 'Poetry Without Tears' by Michael Baldwin, Routledge & Kegan Paul)

58

In the days. of witchcraft, people used to stick pins into images of their enemies, hoping to make them suffer. /

Today there are doctors who stick pins into their patients for the opposite reason—to make them well.

The astonishing // medical practice known as acupuncture—　4(
the word simply means needle puncture—is beginning to be used in England.

You've never / heard of acupuncture? Neither had I—not
till I visited the West End surgery of the only doctor in Eng-
80 land // who practises it on an extensive scale.

'What do you use to cure people by acupuncture?' I asked.

'These', he / said simply, and showed me a handful of needles.
120 Some were gold. Some were silver. Each was only an inch //
127 long. 'Nothing else is needed', he said.

(From the Empire News, 1960)

59.

Seven years, my lord, have now passed since I waited in your
outward rooms, or was repulsed from your door; / during
which time I have been pushing on my work through difficul-
40 ties, of which it is useless to complain, and // have brought it at
last to the verge of publication, without one act of assistance,
one word of encouragement, or / one smile of favour. Such
treatment I did not expect, for I never had a patron before.
80 The shepherd in // Virgil grew at last acquainted with Love,
and found him a native of the rocks.

Is not a patron, my / lord, one who looks with unconcern on
120 a man struggling for life in the water, and when he has reached //
ground, encumbers him with help? The notice which you have
been pleased to take of my labours, had it been / early, had been
kind; but it has been delayed till I am indifferent, and cannot
160 enjoy it; till I am // solitary, and cannot impart it; till I am
known, and do not want it. I hope it is no very / cynical asperity
not to confess obligations where no benefit has been received,
200 or to be unwilling that the public should consider // me as
owing that to a Patron which Providence has enabled me to do
216 for myself.

(From Dr. Samuel Johnson's letter to
Lord Chesterfield, 1755)

86

BUSINESS ENGLISH

The more you study the subject of Business English the more you will realize that it is not a special language. Business English, the English that is used in the everyday activities of the business world, conforms to the same rules and principles of grammar and punctuation as apply to good English anywhere.

Most errors that arise in Business English are caused by a lack of understanding of the parts of speech. Most of us cringe at the mention of such words as noun, pronoun, verb, adverb, preposition, conjunction. Actually, we are using these in our everyday speech. However, we rely upon our judgment to guide us in the correct usage of these words. Yet a simple knowledge of these parts of speech will eliminate the necessity of relying on 'guesswork' and will supplant it with a knowledge of 'right and wrong' in English. Therefore, the purpose of this chapter is to acquaint you with the parts of speech and their correct usage.

NOUNS

A noun is a word that is used to name people, things, ideas, conditions, qualities, emotions, and places. Nouns actually form pictures of the word in the mind. However, some of these pictures we can identify by any of the five senses, and others we cannot. Those we can identify by any of the five senses we call concrete nouns, and those we cannot, we call abstract nouns.

ABSTRACT NOUNS	CONCRETE NOUNS
truth	man
judgment	paper
success	typewriter
patriotism	book
accuracy	letter
courage	desk
power	boy
initiative	house

Concrete nouns can further be broken down into two categories: proper nouns and common nouns. Common nouns refer to a general name for all the objects, places, or persons in a group. Proper nouns refer to a specific object, place, or person in a general group. Proper nouns are always given an initial capital letter.

COMMON NOUNS	PROPER NOUNS
city	London
boy	John
shorthand	Speedwriting
country	Mexico
governor	Mr. Jones
dog	Fido

To form the plural of most nouns, simply add *s*.

receipt	receipts
piece	pieces
cigarette	cigarettes
group	groups
town	towns
crowd	crowds
desk	desks
paper	papers

When the singular form ends in the sound *s*, *sh*, or *ch* the, plural is formed by adding *es*.

glass	glasses
church	churches
pouch	pouches
lunch	lunches
bush	bushes
gas	gases
bench	benches

When common nouns end in *y* and are preceded by a vowel (a, e, i, o, u) add *s* to form the plural. However, if the *y* is preceded by a consonant you change the *y* to *i* and add *es* to form the plural.

valley	valleys
trolley	trolleys
baby	babies
company	companies
play	plays
lady	ladies
tray	trays
berry	berries

In most cases, when a noun ends in *o* and is preceded by a consonant, add *es* to form the plural. When the *o* is preceded by a vowel, merely add *s* to form the plural.

tomato	tomatoes
cargo	cargoes
studio	studios
portfolio	portfolios
potato	potatoes
patio	patios
radio	radios

Many nouns ending in *f* or *fe* form their plurals by changing *f* to *v* and adding *es*.

half	halves
shelf	shelves
knife	knives
leaf	leaves
thief	thieves

Certain nouns have special plural forms.

crisis	crises
alumnus (men)	alumni
alumna (women)	alumnae
basis	bases
medium	media
phenomenon	phenomena

Certain old English nouns have irregular plural forms.

ox	oxen
child	children
man	men
woman	women

When a compound noun is written solid, form the plural by making the last syllable plural.

saleswoman	saleswomen
stockholder	stockholders
workman	workmen
letterhead	letterheads
grandchild	grandchildren
bookcase	bookcases
courthouse	courthouses
classmate	classmates

When forming the plural of compound nouns that are written with hyphens, make the principal noun plural.

court-martial	courts-martial
brother-in-law	brothers-in-law
editor-in-chief	editors-in-chief
mother-in-law	mothers-in-law
sister-in-law	sisters-in-law

COLLECTIVE NOUNS

A noun that is used to denote a group of objects or persons is called a collective noun.

jury	class
committee	audience
faculty	crew
regiment	staff
crowd	group

When a collective noun is singular in meaning, the predicate must also be singular. When a collective noun is plural in meaning, the predicate must also be plural.

The *crew is* standing at attention. (singular)

The *crew have been* assigned duties aboard ship. (plural)

When the sense of the sentence tells you that the individuals described by the collective noun are acting individually, the collective noun is used in a plural sense.

The *class have* failed to agree. i.e. among themselves

The *class has* failed to agree to the new time table. i.e. outside of themselves

91

A possessive noun is a noun which is used to show authorship, possession, origin, or other forms of relationship. When a noun shows any of the above relationships, you must use an apostrophe. The correct placing of the apostrophe is important.

In order to write the possessive noun in the correct form, you must first ascertain whether that noun is singular or plural. Though the easiest way to recognize a plural noun is to see if it ends in *s*, remember that there are some plural nouns which have special forms and do not end in *s*.

For example:

men   children

women   oxen

When you are sure that the noun is in the possessive case, you can write the correct possessive form by following one of the following rules:

The possessive forms of singular nouns are usually formed by adding the apostrophe and *s*.

The *boy's* book is at home.

My *brother's* car is damaged.

The *company's* policy was clear.

Some singular nouns, however, end in the sound *s* and in order to eliminate a succession of *s* or *z* sounds that would cause difficulty in pronouncing, it is permissible to form the possessive by merely adding the apostrophe.

For your *conscience'* sake, do not give up.

For *goodness'* sake, don't do that.

To form the possessive case of plural nouns not ending in *s*, add the apostrophe and *s*.

The *women's* department is closed on Saturday.

The *children's* parents accompanied them.

To form the possessive of plural nouns ending in *s*, just place the apostrophe after the *s*.

The *students'* parents were invited.

The neighbouring *towns'* courthouses are all of brick.

A singular noun that consists of one syllable and ends in *ss* forms its possessive by adding the apostrophe and *s*.

The *class's* record was spotless.

The *glass's* edge was chipped.

A singular noun that consists of two or more syllables and ends in *ss* forms its possessive by adding the apostrophe.

For *goodness'* sake, don't do that.

Possessive nouns that denote time often use the apostrophe to show the omission of a preposition.

The man had ten *years'* experience.

(The man had ten *years of* experience.)

The teacher had three *days'* work left.

(The teacher had three *days of* work left.)

The boy had two *hours'* homework each day.

(The boy had two *hours of* homework each day.)

PRONOUNS

A pronoun is a word that is used in place of a noun. You can readily see how necessary a pronoun is when you try to write a paragraph without using one.

WITHOUT PRONOUNS

Mr. Jones dictated to *Mr. Jones's* secretary.
The book reached *the book's* destination.
The boy spoke to *the boy's* mother.
The plant reached *the plant's* maximum growth.

WITH PRONOUNS

Mr. Jones dictated to *his* secretary.
The book reached *its* destination.
The boy spoke to *his* mother.
The plant reached *its* maximum growth.

The incorrect usage of pronouns, however, is just as awkward as the complete lack of use of pronouns. It is necessary to separate the pronouns into four groups: personal, indefinite, interrogative, and relative.

93

A personal pronoun is one which lets you know by its form if it represents the speaker, the person spoken to, or the person spoken of. The personal pronouns are: *I, you, he, she, it,* with their declensions.

Depending upon how they are used in a sentence, pronouns have different forms. Study the forms in the table below. This table is called a declension.

PERSONAL PRONOUNS

Singular

	1st person	*2nd person*	*3rd person*
Nominative	I	you	he, she, it
Possessive	my, mine	your, yours	his, her, hers, its
Objective	me	you	him, her, it

Plural

Nominative	we	you	they
Possessive	our, ours	your, yours	their, theirs
Objective	us	you	them

There are no apostrophes in the personal pronouns.

INDEFINITE PRONOUNS

Indefinite pronouns are pronouns that do not name any particular individual or thing. Some of these are: *each, every, everyone, either, neither, no one, nobody, everybody,* and *anybody.* When using these pronouns they must be referred to by a *singular* pronoun because they are singular in number.

Incorrect:

Neither John nor Mary *are* going.

Everyone does *their* work well.

Correct:

Neither John nor Mary *is* going.

Everyone does *his* work well.

94

A relative pronoun is used to connect its antecedent to a subordinate clause.

This is the man *who* built our house.

(This is the man *and* he built our house.)

Notice that the word *who* takes the place of *and he*. It replaces *he* which is the subject of *built* (who built?), and it connects the dependent clause to the antecedent *man*.

The relative pronouns are *who*, *which*, *what*, and *that*, with their declined forms. The clause that the relative pronoun introduces is called a relative clause.

When you refer to a person, use *who*. When you refer to an animal or inanimate object, use *which*. *That* is used to refer to all three, as a more general term.

WHO—WHOM

If you memorize just a few words, you will have no trouble choosing the correct word. Use *whom* after the following words or prepositions:

at	by
of	to
except	toward
with	than

This is Mr. Jones, *than whom* there is no better salesman.

At whom did he direct his remarks?

This is the person *to whom* I wrote.

By whom was he introduced?

Here is the man *with whom* we made the contract.

Whom is also used when it is the object of the verb.

Whom do you expect? (expect whom?)

The firm *whom* we billed had an excellent credit rating. (billed whom?)

Who is used when it is the subject of the verb.

Who is he? (subject of verb *is*)

I did not know *who* he was. (subject of verb *was*)

The choice of *that* or *which* is easily made if you keep in mind this rule: *That* is appropriate to defining clauses, and *which* to non-defining clauses.

The story *that* we read in class was interesting.

The story of the shipwreck, *which* we read in class, was interesting.

Notice that in the first sentence we make use of *that* to define the specific story that was read. However, in the second sentence, the particular story is already identified, and we are merely giving extra information—namely that we read it in class.

In most cases, the *which* clause is set off by commas, and the *that* clause is not

INTERROGATIVE PRONOUNS

Pronouns that are used to ask questions are called interrogative pronouns. They are: *which*, *who*, and *what*.

Use *who* if the interrogative pronoun is the subject of the sentence. (Nominative case)

Who is there?

Who is the new owner?

Who threw the ball?

The possessive case of *who* is *whose*.

Whose book is this?

Whose brother is he?

Whose watch was broken?

Remember: The word *whose* does not have an apostrophe. *Who's* is the contraction of *who is*.

The objective case of *who* is *whom*. It must be used when the interrogative pronoun is the object of the verb.

Whom did you call?

VERBS

A verb is used to denote action, being, or state of being.

It is necessary to mention here that a sentence is composed of two parts: the subject and the predicate, which together express a complete thought.

The boy ran home. (*The boy* is the subject of the sentence and *ran home* is the predicate.)

It is easy to find the verb in the above sentence. Remember, the verb expresses action, and in the above sentence the verb is the word *ran*. To find the subject of the sentence, ask the question, *Who?* or *What?* before the verb; as *Who ran? The boy ran....* Therefore, *The boy* is the subject.

THE TENSE OF VERBS

The tense of a verb is the form of a verb which denotes the time of an action or an event. The tenses of a verb are past, present, and future, depending upon the time they express. These are called the primary tenses.

Past Tense: He *worked* very hard.
Present Tense: He *works* very hard.
Future Tense: He *will work* very hard.

THE PAST TENSE

The past tense should be used when reference is made to a definite past event or action.

I *went* to the cinema when I was in the city.
I *sold* the book last year.

THE PRESENT TENSE

The present tense is used to denote action going on at the present time.

I *am* satisfied.
He *is* here.

The present tense is used to indicate that action is continued or habitual.

I *see* him every day.
We *sell* hardware.

The present tense is used to denote a general truth.

Snakes *are* reptiles.
Sugar *is* sweet.

97

The future tense denotes what will take place at a future time.

I *shall visit* you in an hour.

We *shall be* there tomorrow.

They *will continue* the service next week.

SHALL—WILL

Two points are taken into consideration when deciding between these two words. First, the person of the subject (first, second, third); second, whether the sentence expresses simple futurity, determination, or promise.

Simple futurity refers to action still to come, just as the past tense refers to action finished in the past. To indicate simple futurity with a subject in the first person, such as *I* or *we*, use *shall*.

I *shall* shave later.

I *shall* be there tomorrow.

We *shall* go soon.

We *shall* return in a week.

To indicate simple futurity with a subject in the second or third person, such as *you, she, he, it*, or *they*, use *will*.

She *will* return later.

He *will* be there tomorrow.

They *will* go soon.

It *will* be sunny tomorrow.

When you wish to express determination or promise, just reverse the rule for simple futurity. To indicate determination or promise in the first person use *will*. To indicate determination or promise in the second or third person use *shall*.

I *will* be there tomorrow.

They *shall* go soon.

He *shall* visit you next week.

We *will* return.

As you can see from the sentence, *I will be there tomorrow*, more than a mere intention or desire is expressed. You are actually assuming an obligation or making a promise.

Follow the same rules that you applied to *shall* and *will* to *should* and *would*. With the first person subjects use *should* to express simple futurity; use *would* to express determination, or promise.

I *should be* finished by tomorrow.

With second or third person subject use *should* to express determination or promise, and *would* to express simple futurity.

You *would like* the glasses if you would try them.

When you wish to express obligation, use *should* with all three persons.

I *should visit* him.

They *should send* a letter.

You *should return* the book.

Notice that in these cases, *should* has the meaning of *ought to*. Use *would* to express habitual action in all three persons.

He *would* always be late.

THE PERFECT TENSES

To represent completed action or state of being, there are three verb phrases which are called perfect tenses. The perfect tenses are: the present perfect, the past perfect, and the future perfect.

PRESENT PERFECT TENSE

The present perfect tense is used to denote a condition or action begun in the past and continued to the present. To form the present perfect tense of a verb, use the past participle preceded by *have* or *has*.

I *have sent* for the book.

They *have gone* away.

Notice that the helping verb *have* is used in all cases in the present perfect tense with one exception. When the subject is third person singular use *has*.

He *has* gone.

They *have* gone.

It *has* gone.

That *has* gone.

PAST PERFECT TENSE

This tense is used to denote that the action of the verb was completed at some definite time in the past. To form the past perfect tense, the helping verb *had* is used with the perfect participle.

He *had left* by the time I arrived.

He *had hidden* the prizes before the children entered the room.

FUTURE PERFECT TENSE

Use the future perfect tense to express action to be completed before some other future action takes place, or to express action that is to be completed at some definite future time. To form the future perfect tense use the helping verb phrases *shall have* and *will have*.

He *will have* finished the work by three o'clock.

I *shall have* left by that time.

INFINITIVES

Infinitives are verb forms which make no assertion, but indicate in a general way a state of being or an action. The infinitive is easily identified by the word *to*, which can be expressed or understood.

To swim well requires good breathing.

To write is fun.

THE SPLIT INFINITIVE

The split infinitive is nothing more than the separation of the word *to* from its verb. This is not good form and can easily be rectified by finding another way to frame the same thought.

Poor Form: To clearly define the steps is our aim.

Good Form: To define the steps clearly is our aim.

Poor Form: I want to clearly understand each step.

Good Form: I want to understand clearly each step.

Repeat the preposition *to* before each member of a series of infinitive phrases.

His orders stated that he was *to* clear the grounds, *to* build the houses, and *to* arrange for the landscaping.

100

ADJECTIVES

An adjective is a word used to modify a noun or a pronoun. It defines, limits, or describes the noun or pronoun which it modifies.

Compare these two advertisements. Which do you think will arouse a prospective employer's interest more?

Woman, college education, looking for job as secretary in theatrical field.

Attractive, energetic, young woman, college education and experience, desires challenging position as secretary to overburdened executive in theatrical field.

The simple form of an adjective is known as the positive form. When the adjective carries the meaning of more or less, it is called the comparative form. The superlative form carries the meaning of most or least.

If a positive adjective ends with the letter *e*, simply add *r* to form the comparative form, and *st* for the superlative form.

Positive	Comparative	Superlative
fine	finer	finest
vile	viler	vilest
late	later	latest

When an adjective ends with *y* preceded by a consonant, change *y* to *i* and add *er* to form the comparative form, and *est* to form the superlative form.

Positive	Comparative	Superlative
funny	funnier	funniest
merry	merrier	merriest
happy	happier	happiest
busy	busier	busiest
tiny	tinier	tiniest
lazy	lazier	laziest

To form the comparative or superlative of a one-syllable adjective that ends with one consonant preceded by one vowel, double the final consonant and add *er* or *est*.

Positive	Comparative	Superlative
trim	trimmer	trimmest
hot	hotter	hottest
sad	sadder	saddest

When forming the comparative or superlative of an adjective of two or more syllables it is better to use *more* for the comparative and *most* for the superlative.

Positive	*Comparative*	*Superlative*
grateful	more grateful	most grateful
difficult	more difficult	most difficult
durable	more durable	most durable

Remember! The comparative form is used only when comparing two objects or persons. The superlative form is used when comparing three or more objects or persons.

ADVERBS

An adverb is a word used to modify a verb, an adjective, or another adverb. An adverb answers the question, *How, When,* or *Where.*

He *quickly* ran home. (Adverb modifying verb *ran*)

It is an *extremely narrow street.* (Adverb modifying adjective *narrow*)

He walked *very* slowly. (Adverb modifying adverb *slowly*)

It is important that you watch the placing of the adverb in the sentence. From the following sentences, you can see how the placing of the adverb can change the meaning of the sentence. As a general rule, write it just before the word it modifies.

Only I saw him.

I *only* saw him.

I saw *only* him.

I saw him *only.*

Do not use an adjective in place of an adverb. An adjective modifies a noun or pronoun. An adverb modifies a verb, an adjective, or another adverb.

PREPOSITIONS

Prepositions are words that are used to connect a following noun or pronoun with another word or phrase in the sentence.

They presented the medal *to* him *at* the meeting *of* the officials.

102

The following is a list of common prepositions:

about	across	after
along	among	at
before	behind	beside
between	by	concerning
during	except	for
from	in	into
of	on	over
throughout	till	to
towards	until	up
upon	with	without

Some word groups are used as prepositions.

apart from	contrary to
as to	in reference to
in addition to	as regards
with regard to	in accordance with
as for	on account of

FROM—THAN

The word *than* is not a preposition and cannot be used as such. In most cases this mistake is made after the word *different* and *differently*.

This book is *different from* the one I read.

Do the work *differently from* the way you did it in the past.

UNNECESSARY PREPOSITIONS

Do not use unnecessary prepositions. The most common error of this kind is the placing of the unnecessary preposition at the end of a sentence.

Incorrect: I cannot stop *from* laughing.

Correct: I cannot stop laughing.

Incorrect: Where did he put it *at*?

Correct: Where did he put it?

Do not use the word *of* after the word *all* unless it is followed by a pronoun.

    Incorrect: All of the boys went home.
    Correct: All the boys went home.
    Correct: All of them went home.

BESIDE—BESIDES

The word *beside* means along side of; the word *besides* means also, or in addition to, or moreover.

    He stood *beside* me.
    How many days *besides* today have you been away?

BETWEEN—AMONG

The word *between* refers to two; the word *among* refers to more than two.

    He will divide the work *between* the two of us.
    He will divide the work *among* the class.

USE OF *of* AFTER *both*

Do not use the word *of* after the word *both* unless a pronoun follows it.

    • Incorrect: *Both of* the orders went astray.
    Correct: Both orders went astray.
    Correct: *Both of* us went to the show.

CONJUNCTIONS

A co-ordinate conjunction is a word used to connect words, phrases, and clauses, of equal rank.

    Bring me the letter *and* the envelope.
    The letter was sent from London *or* from Manchester.
    The typing was fast, *but* the accuracy was poor.

A co-ordinate conjunction is also used to join elements of the same rank or grammatical relation.

    The dealer *buys and sells* used cars. (Compound verb)
    Pens and pencils are sold at the shop. (Compound subject)

A correlative conjunction is a conjunction that is used in pairs only. Some of these are:

both—and, not only—but also. neither—nor, whether—or, either—or

Both Charles *and* Mary went to the country.

Neither Charles *nor* Mary went to the country.

A subordinate conjunction connects groups of words of unequal rank. Some of these conjunctions are:

when, because, while, after, if, although

He went to the country *because* the weather was sultry.

They went to dinner *after* they saw the show.

THE SENTENCE

As we mentioned previously, the sentence is a group of words which expresses a complete thought. Sentences may be divided into three categories: declarative, interrogative, and imperative.

A declarative sentence states a fact or makes an assertion.

You send your examination in the enclosed envelope.

An interrogative sentence asks a question. It is always followed by a question mark.

Did you send your examination to us?

An imperative sentence expresses a command.

Send it now.

In order to express a complete thought, the sentence must consist of a subject and a predicate. The subject is the word or words about which something is said. The predicate is the word or group of words that does the telling.

Mary reads.

Mary is the subject and *reads* is the predicate. Of course, most sentences consist of more than two words. However, these two words are the bare subject and the bare predicate. Any other words in a sentence will merely expand or modify the meaning of the bare subject and the bare predicate, and these words are called modifiers. The bare subject with all its modifiers is called the complete subject. The bare predicate with all its modifiers is called the complete predicate.

A large *stock* of cameras, flash bulbs, screens, and tripods *is* carried at all times.

The word *stock* is the bare subject. The phrase, 'A large stock of cameras, flash bulbs, screens, and tripods,' is the complete subject because all the other words in that phrase modify the bare subject. 'Is carried at all times,' is the complete predicate.

It is necessary for you to be able to find the bare subject and bare predicate of a sentence to make sure that the predicate agrees with the subject in number. If the subject is singular, the predicate must be singular. If you can recognize the bare subject you will have no trouble in selecting the right form for the bare predicate.

CLAUSES

Often you will come across a group of words which contains a subject and a predicate but does not express a complete thought. This is called a clause.

Since my book is torn, I will replace it.

Although 'Since my book is torn,' contains a subject, *book*, and a predicate, *is torn*, it is not a sentence because it does not express a complete thought, nor would it be clear if written alone.

THE PARAGRAPH

A paragraph is a sentence or group of sentences which tends to set off one idea, or the development of that idea. The well-constructed paragraph usually consists of anywhere from four to ten lines. This, however, does not apply to the first paragraph of a letter, which should be a short one. A short paragraph which is easy to see and easy to grasp, speeds its subject into the reader's mind. It is an indication of what you are going to write about. You will agree that a letter which contains few or no paragraphs is not inviting to the eye. On the other hand, too many paragraphs are just as unappealing. When you bear in mind the fact that a paragraph is supposed to give the reader a chance to 'catch his breath' and to 'grasp' the contents of the letter in a logical sequence, you will have no trouble in making your paragraphs at just the right point.

RUN-ON SENTENCES

A run-on sentence is a sentence that is made by writing two or more statements together as though they were one. It is more correct to place a conjunction immediately after the first complete thought, or to insert a full stop after it.

Incorrect: The rain began to fall, I put on my raincoat.
Correct: The rain began to fall, so I put on my raincoat.
Correct: The rain began to fall. I put on my raincoat.

In the above sentence, the correction was made by placing a full stop after the first complete thought.

SENTENCE FRAGMENTS

A sentence fragment is just the opposite of the run-on sentence, made by writing part of a sentence for a whole one.

Incorrect: Having written to you last month. I expected to hear from you by now.
Correct: Having written to you last month, I expected to have heard from you by now.

UNRELATED PHRASES

If an adjectival phrase begins a sentence, it should clearly relate to the subject of the sentence.

At the age of four, Mary's mother died.

This sentence implies that Mary's mother was four years old when she died. The sentence may be corrected as follows:

At the age of four, Mary lost her mother.

DOUBLE NEGATIVE

One negative word is all that is necessary to express an idea of negation. When you put a second negative in a sentence, it cancels the first, making the sentence positive. Therefore, avoid using the double negative.

Incorrect: I do not have no time.
Correct: I do not have any time.

PUNCTUATION

Use a capital letter to begin every sentence.

I must go home.

How are you?

Use a capital to begin a direct quotation:.

He said, 'My father is at home.'

She answered, 'Let's visit him.'

Use capitals to begin all proper nouns.

I saw Mr. Jones today.

My brother is in Liverpool.

Use capitals for the names of holidays.

He will be home from school during his Christmas holidays.

The girls all bought new dresses for Easter.

Use capitals for North, East, South, or West, if they designate certain sections of the country.

He was brought up in the South.

The winter in North Alaska is unbearable.

Use capitals for the names of organizations and institutions.

His membership of the Metropolitan Club expired.

He was a member of the Medical Club.

Use capitals for trade names.

He completed his course in Speedwriting.

He bought a new Ford.

Titles should begin with capital letters when they take the place of names.

The Colonel was here today.

Say hello to Mother.

Titles of books may be written entirely in capital letters.

A STORY OF OUR ISLAND was used as a text.

THE LASTING PEACE is now on sale.

108

Use the full stop at the end of a sentence that makes a statement.

It rained today.

I am going home.

Use a full stop after abbreviations and initials.

Mr., Co., Ltd., Herts.

Use three stops to show a break in a quotation:

He said, 'He gained fame, money . . . but died in poverty.'

COMMA

Words in a series should be separated by commas, except where a conjunction is used.

John will take the note, the contract and the lease to Mr. Brown.

You may leave the letter, the paper or the book at my office.

Phrases used in a series should be separated by commas.

The lad called on Mr. Short, on his mother, and on a friend.

You can make payment by money order, by cheque, or in cash.

Clauses used in a series should be separated by commas.

Mr. Jones went to his home, picked up his evening paper and was in his favourite chair before dinner.

Words used to address a person should be set off by commas.

No, Mr. Jones, the cheque was not sent out.

I am certain, my friends, that the bill was passed.

Use a comma to set off an introductory or modifying clause from the principal clause of the sentence.

If you cannot come at this time, please call me on the telephone.

When you have completed your examination, I should like to see you in my office.

An introductory adverbial phrase is usually followed' by a comma.

In order to avoid delay, wire us tonight.

A clause that is not needed to complete the thought of the main clause is set off by commas. (This is an 'unnecessary' clause.)

> Miss Bradshaw, who is head of personnel, will not be at her desk tomorrow.

A clause that is needed to complete the meaning of the main clause is not set off by commas. (This is a 'necessary' clause.)

> The goods that you ordered were on the train today.

Parenthetical expressions, such as *nevertheless, in fact, however, therefore, of course*, which do not destroy the meaning of the sentence, are usually set off by commas.

> He will, of course, return the book to the library.

Use commas to set off a word or phrase that explains a preceding term.

> His father, Mr. John Brown, was nominated for office.

A comma sets off a question which is added to a statement.

> You sent the letter, did you not?

Use a comma before the abbreviation *etc.* and after it except when it ends a sentence.

> Have with you pen, pencil, paper, etc., when you come to class.

Use commas to separate parts of addresses, geographical names, and dates, whether in a statement or address on an envelope.

> We arrived at 22 Park Lane, Bradford, Yorks., on June 25.

COLON

A colon is used to introduce a list of things.

> Mr. Jones asked the new secretary to bring the following things: writing paper, pencils, a blotter, and a dust cloth.

Use a colon to introduce a quotation of special significance.

> The Chairman made the following statement: 'Our country has reched the crossroads. . . .'

SEMICOLON

Separate the independent clauses of a sentence by a semicolon if no connecting word is used between the clauses.

> Just post the enclosed card; postage is pre-paid.

QUESTION MARK

Use a question mark after each direct question.

May I see him?

How do you feel?

The question mark should be used after individual members of a series, each of which might be expanded into a complete sentence.

Who is the mayor of Halifax? of Bury? of Dewsbury?

Use the question mark in parentheses to denote uncertainty or doubt as to the facts.

The parcel was sent on March 23 (?) by parcel post.

EXCLAMATION MARK

Use the exclamation mark after a word, a clause, or a sentence to denote emotion.

Oh! Alas!

What a beautiful day!

QUOTATION MARKS

Use quotation marks to enclose direct quotations.

He said, 'I am sure you will be happy.'

Use quotation marks to enclose words to which direct reference is made.

There are too many 'ifs' in the letter.

Use quotation marks to enclose words that are somewhat unusual.

He is a 'square shooter.'

Quotation marks are placed outside the comma or full stop, but inside the semicolon and colon.

APOSTROPHE

Use the apostrophe to form contractions of certain words.

He won't be home today, because he wasn't able to complete his business in time.

It is better to write the words in full except in a direct quotation of speech.

Use the apostrophe to show the possessive form of a word.

It was John's book.

He is Mary's cousin.

111

The hyphen is used to divide a word at the end of a line.

Do not make any movements that will prove unnecessary.

The hyphen is used to connect two or more separate words which combine to form a compound word.

In no time at all he became editor-in-chief.

She visited her mother-in-law.

A hyphen is used between two words which combine to form a single adjective *before* a noun. Note that the hyphen is not used if the noun precedes the adjective.

He believed in high-pressure selling.

His selling technique employed high pressure.

DASH

Use the dash to separate two parts of a sentence when there is a complete break in the thought. They act like parentheses, and the words between them could be omitted without altering the sentence.

The large house—and make no mistake, it was large—was completely demolished by the fire.

Use the dash to indicate the omission of letters or figures.

He was telephoned by Mr. R—.

PARENTHESES

Use the parentheses to set off words or expressions that have only a slight bearing upon the thought of the sentence.

The last time I visited you (March 23) I left my brief-case with the secretary.

Use parentheses to set off the number or letter of each item included in a list.

This is what has been completed:
(1) The living room
(2) The kitchen
(3) The hallway

WORDS FREQUENTLY CONFUSED

Accept means to agree to receive.
Except means to leave out.
   June will *accept* this gift.
   We shall post all items *except* glass.

Their refers to individuals.
There refers to a place.
   All the pupils returned *their* books.
   He will go *there* to study.

Its is possessive.
It's indicates the omission of a letter—short form for *it is.*
   The company sent *its* order.
   It's time to dispatch the order.

Further refers to time, quantity, or degree.
Farther refers to distance or space.
   I have no *further* wishes at present.
   Tomorrow we shall go *farther.*

Already means previously.
All ready means completely ready.
   The book was *already* published.
   She was *all ready* for the dance.

Past or an adjective is used as a noun denoting former time.
Passed refers to an action.
   We have seen him in the *past.*
   The procession *passed* here today.

Advise means to give counsel.
Advice means the counsel given or received.
   Please *advise* me what to do.
   Please take my *advice.*

Than refers to comparison.
Then means next, or at that time.
   It is easier said *than* done.
   First he went to the store and *then* he went home.

Precede means to go before.
Proceed means to go on, or to continue.
   The *preceding* paragraph introduced the subject clearly.
   They will *proceed* with the trial after the adjournment.

Affect means to impress or influence.
Effect refers to outcome or result.
   His presence will not *affect* the decision.
   The *effects* of the action were felt by everyone.

Personal means private.
Personnel refers to employees.
   He considered his marriage a *personal* affair.
   The manpower shortage caused a critical *personnel* prob-
      lem.

Formerly means in time past.
Formally means according to set rules or convention.
   He *formerly* represented the Jackson Company.
   He was *formally* introduced to the group.

Principle refers to basic doctrine or rule.
Principal refers to highest in rank.
   His actions were not in accordance with the *principles* of
      conduct.
   He was the *principal* speaker on the programme.

Stationery refers to those articles sold by stationers.
Stationary means fixed in a certain place.
   He bought *stationery* for the office.
   They fired at *stationary* targets.

Hanged refers to a person.
Hung refers to an article.
   He was *hanged* at dawn.
   The picture was *hung* above the chair.

Act as means to take the part of.
Act like means to imitate.
   I shall *act as* director during Mr. Johnson's holiday.
   He *acted like* a stranger.

Adapt means to make suitable.
Adept means expert.
Adopt means to make one's property.
   The children *adapt* themselves to the classroom.
   They are *adept* at finding things to do.
   They *adopt* the habits of the other school children.

Adverse means contrary.
Averse means unwilling.
   The trip was cancelled because of *adverse* weather.
   They were *averse* to taking the trip.

You *agree on* a plan.
You *agree to* a proposition.
You *agree with* another person.
   The generals *agreed on* the strategy.
   They *agreed to* discuss other means.
   They *agreed with* one another.

Altogether means completely.
All together means as a group.
   You are *altogether* mistaken.
   They will meet at the park and go *all together*.

You are *angry with* a person.
You are *angry about* something. (Never use *angry at*.)
   She was very *agry with* him.
   She was *angry about* his tardiness.

As . . . as is used after a positive expression.
So . . . as is used after a negative expression.
   They were *as* lucky *as* they expected to be.
   They were not *so* lucky *as* they expected to be.

Beside means next to.
Besides means moreover or in addition to.
   Put the chair *beside* the desk.
   He had other means of getting there *besides* those he mentioned.

115

Bound means under legal or moral restraint.
Determined means self-decided.
Under the terms of the contract he was *bound* to return.
He was *determined* to return.

Can shows ability.
May shows permission.
I *can* write shorthand.
May I go with you?

Common means shared by many.
Mutual means exchanged.
Poor spelling is a *common* weakness.
The feeling of friendship was *mutual*.

Compare with refers to two objects in the same category.
Compare to refers to two objects in different categories.
Compare this test *with* the last one.
They *compared* him *to* a mad dog.

WORDS REQUIRING SPECIAL PREPOSITIONS

abhorrence of	adhere to
adapted to or for	dependent on
affinity between	confer on
affinity with	confer with
affinity to	conversant with
comply with	independent of
confide in	hatred of
confide to	reconcile to
correspond to	reconcile with
correspond with	part from
absolve from	part with

116

WORDS COMMONLY MISSPELLED

A

ab-sorp-tion
ac-cel-er-ate
ac-ces-si-ble
ac-ces-sory
ac-ci-den-tally
ac-com-mo-date
ac-com-mo-da-tion
ac-cu-mu-late
achieve-ment
ac-knowl-edg-ment
ac-quaint-ance
ac-qui-esce
ad-journ-ment

af-fect
af-fili-ate
all right
al-lege
al-lot-ment
al-ready
alu-mi-nium
amend-ment
ana-lyze
antarc-tic
apos-tro-phe
ap-pa-ra-tus
ap-par-ent

ap-pear-ance
ap-point-ment
ap-pro-pri-ate
ar-range-ment
asi-nine
as-sign-ment
as-sist-ance
as-ter-isk
ath-let-ics
at-tend-ance
at-tor-neys
au-di-ble
aux-il-iary

B

bal-lot
ba-na-na
bank-ruptcy
bar-ba-rous

bat-tal-ion
bene-fi-cial
bene-fited
budg-et

buoy-ant
bu-reaux
busi-ness

C

cal-en-dar
cam-paign
can-cel-la-tion
car-bu-rettor
ca-tas-tro-phe
ceil-ing
ceme-tery
chauf-feur
col-lege

co-los-sal
com-mit-ment
com-mit-tee
con-cede
con-fi-dent
con-science
con-sci-en-tious
con-sec-u-tively

con-sen-sus
con-spicu-ous
con-tro-versy
cor-ru-gated
coun-cil (a group)
coun-sel (advice)
cyl-in-der
cyn-ic-al

D

de-fend-ant
de-ferred
defi-nite
deuce
de-vel-op

de-vel-op-ment
diph-the-ria
dis-ap-pear
dis-ap-point

dis-crep-ancy
dis-sat-is-fied
di-vine
dom-i-nance

E

ec-sta-sy
ef-fect
eli-gi-ble
e-lim-i-nate
em-bar-rass

em-i-nent
en-dorse-ment
en-ter-prise
en-velop
en-vel-op-ment

ev-i-dently
ex-haust
ex-hi-bi-tion
ex-ist-ence
ex-traor-di-nary

F

fa-mil-iar
fea-si-ble
Feb-ru-ary
fiend

fier-y
flexi-ble
for-ci-ble
forth-right

forty
four-some
fran-chise

G

gauge
gnaw-ing
gov-ern-ment

gov-er-nor
gram-mar

griev-ous
gym-na-sium

H

hap-haz-ard
heart-rend-ing
hæm-or-rhage

hin-drance
home-ly

hy-giene
hy-poc-ri-sy

I

id-i-osyn-cra-sy
il-le-gal
il-lit-er-ate
imi-ta-tion
im-me-di-ately
in-au-gu-rate
in-ci-den-tally

in-del-ible
in-de-pend-ence
in-flam-m-able
in-hab-it-ant
in-stal-la-tion
in-ter-cede

in-ter-fere
in-ter-fered
in-vei-gle
ir-rel-e-vant
ir-re-sisti-ble
is-suing

J

jour-ney

jus-ti-fi-able

K

ki-mo-no

knowl-edge

118

L

labo-ra-tory
le-giti-mate
liq-uefy

liq-ue-fac-tion
live-li-hood
lone-li-ness

loose (adjective)
lose (verb)
lovely

M

main-te-nance
man-age-ment
ma-nœu-vre

man-ual
mathe-mat-ics

mile-age
mur-mur

N

nec-es-sary
ne-ces-sity
nickel

nine-teenth
ninety
ninth

no-tice-able
no-to-ri-ety
now-a-days

O

oc-ca-sion
oc-ca-sion-ally
oc-curred

oc-cur-rence
omis-sion

one-self
op-po-site

P

pag-eant
pam-phlet
para-chute
par-al-lel
par-lia-men-tar-y
pas-teur-ize
peace-able
pe-cul-iar
per-ma-nent
per-mis-si-ble
per-son-ally
per-suade
phy-si-cian

pla-gi-arism
play-wright
pos-ses-sion
po-ta-to
prai-rie
pre-cede
pre-ced-ing
pre-cious
pref-er-able
pre-limi-nary
pre-sump-tu-ous
preva-lent

prin-ci-pal (chief)
prin-ci-ple (rule)
privi-lege
pro-ce-dure
pro-ceed
pro-fes-sor
promi-nent
pro-nun-ci-ation
proph-e-cy (prediction)
proph-e-sy (to predict)
pub-lic-ly
pur-sue
pur-su-ing

Q

ques-tion-naire

119

R

re-ceipt
re-ceive
re-cipi-ent
rec-om-mend
rec-om-men-da-tion
ref-er-ence
re-ferred
rele-vant

re-lief
re-nown
re-pel-lent
re-plies
re-scind
res-tau-rant
re-veal

rhap-sody
rheto-ric
rhu-barb
rhyme
rhythm
ri-dic-u-lous
ro-ta-ry

S

sac-ri-le-gious
safe-ty
sale-able
scho-las-tic
scis-sors
sec-re-tary
seize
sen-si-ble
sepa-rate
se-rial
shep-herd
ship-ment

shipped
siege
simi-lar
si-mul-ta-ne-ous
since
size-able
sou-ve-nir
sneak
sneer
speech
split-ting
strictly

sub-sidy
suc-ces-sor
suf-fi-cient
su-ing
su-per-in-tend-ent
sur-geon
sur-prise
sus-cep-ti-ble
sus-pi-cious
sym-me-try
syn-ony-mous

T

tan-gi-ble
tar-iff
tem-po-rary
ten-ant

ter-ri-ble
their
too (also)

trag-e-dy
trans-ferred
tyr-anny

U

un-doubt-edly

use-ful

V

vac-ci-nate
vege-ta-ble

vil-lain
vol-ume

W

Wednes-day

weird

WORD CHOICE

A good writer chooses his words with care. His purpose is to express his thought clearly and simply. He will not use a long word when a shorter one expresses his thought. Poor writers often use long words in an effort to impress the reader; good writers do not.

In the following columns are pairs of words similar in meaning, yet with a difference. Look them up in a dictionary to learn the difference, then use them in sentences that you think will clearly express their correct usage.

dishevelled	upset
homogeneous	alike
dispatch	send
conversant	acquainted
ameliorate	better
cognomen	name
chastisement	punishment
virulent	intense
precipitate	hasty
beneficent	good
acclivity	ascent
ambulatory	movable
amanuensis	secretary
blandishment	flattery

WORDS PRONOUNCED ALIKE BUT SPELLED DIFFERENTLY

Many words have the same sound, but are different in spelling and meaning.

so	sew, sow
to	too, two
bow	bough
know	no
knew	new
ought	aught
mail	male

based	baste
pair	pare, pear
course	coarse
hair	hare
grate	great
blew	blue
bear	bare
wear	ware
four	fore
indite	indict
aisle	isle
fur	fir
straight	strait
bail	bale
pail	pale
threw	through
plain	plane
or	ore
heard	herd
aloud	allowed
seams	seems
find	fined
die	dye
lead (metal)	led
root	route
colonel	kernel
groan	grown
scene	seen
berth	birth
metal	mettle
hall	haul
dual	duel
read	red
marshal	martial
hours	ours
peace	piece

WORDS THAT HAVE GROWN TOGETHER

antechamber	eastbound
armchair	farsighted
backdoor	fireproof
bathtub	foolproof
bedroom	foreclosure
bedside	handbook
bedtime	handwriting
beefsteak	henceforward
blackmail	hereafter
blindfold	lawmaker
bookcase	masterpiece
book-keeper	meanwhile
bookmaker	newsagent
broadside	newspaperman
businesslike	playwright
busybody	postmark
bygone	scrapbook
caretaker	tablecloth
classmate	timekeeper
clubhouse	turnover
commonplace	viewpoint
copyright	windstorm
crossroads	worksheet

WORDS SPELLED ALIKE BUT PRONOUNCED DIFFERENTLY

con-*tract* (verb)	tor-*ment* (verb)
con-tract (noun)	*tor*-ment (noun)
close (verb)	sur-*vey* (verb)
close (noun or adjective)	*sur*-vey (noun)
pre-*sent* (verb)	di-*gest* (verb)
pres-ent (noun)	*di*-gest (noun)
ess-*ay* (verb)	con-*test* (verb)
ess-ay (noun)	*con*-test (noun)

con-sum-mate (verb)
con-*sum*-mate (adjective)
per-*mit* (verb)
per-mit (noun)
con-*trast* (verb)
con-trast (noun)
pro-*ject* (verb)
proj-ect (noun)

sub-*ject* (verb)
sub-ject (noun)
in-*sert* (verb)
in-sert (noun)
ob-*ject* (verb)
ob-ject (noun)

TECHNICAL AND FOREIGN WORDS IN COMMON USE

aerial
alternating
arrester
battery
circuit
crystal
dynamo
ether
frequency
impedance
kilowatt
microphone
ohm
condenser
audibility
broadcaster
cathode
counterpoise
detector
elctrolysis
filament
heterodyne
oscillations
polarization
radiation

variometer
carburettor
chassis
speedometer
accelerator
fuselage
psychology
geology
ad valorem
data
bona fide
corps
rectifier
rheostat
stator
transmitter
watt
engine
limousine
tread
gauge
gasket
ailerons
spark
entomology

resistance
selectivity
transformer
vacuum

endocrine
ex officio
carte blanche
clientele
microfilm

TRANSCRIPTION TECHNIQUE

INTRODUCTION TO THE BUSINESS LETTER

The letters that a firm sends are often the only contact between the firm and its customers. It is essential, therefore, that these letters create a favourable impression. A letter that is attractive in appearance is, in a sense, a good-will ambassador, and your ability to type an attractive letter is your 'hallmark' as an efficient, capable typist or secretary.

This section is designed to enable you to produce a perfectly-typed letter. When you have become familiar with the information, you will have a chance to put it to use by typing typical business letters. Before long you will be typing perfect letters automatically.

PARTS OF THE BUSINESS LETTER

A business letter generally contains the following parts:

Letterhead	Complimentary close
Date line	Company name
Inside address	Dictator's name and/or title
Salutation	Reference initials
Body of the letter	

This section will discuss these various parts in detail. Before reading further, however, locate each of these parts on the diagram shown below so that you will be familiar with their postion.

In addition to the more common parts shown above, some letters may also include:

Attention line	Carbon copy notation
Subject or 're' line	Postscript
Enclosure notation	

The position of these additional parts will also be discussed in the following pages.

When studying the various parts of a business letter in the pages that follow, pay particular attention to the vertical spacing —the number of blank lines to be left above and below each part. Except for the space above the inside address, these never vary. Later in this section, when studying punctuation and letter styles, you will learn the proper punctuation to use, and the correct horizontal positioning.

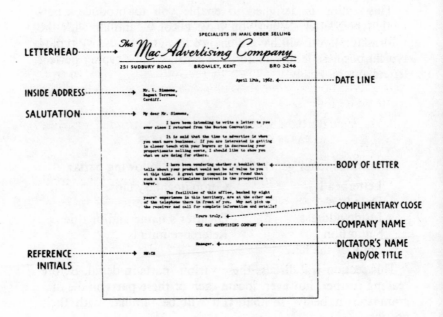

128

The letterhead is the stationery used by a company for its correspondence. The printed material at the top of the page usually contains the firm's name, address, and telephone number. It may also contain a company slogan and the names of the executives of the firm. This printed material normally occupies approximately two inches at the top of the page (12 lines.)

DATE LINE

The horizontal positioning of the date line—whether ranged left, centred, or ranged right—depends upon the letter style used. The variation of its position on the line will be explained as each letter style is shown in the following pages. In every letter style, however, the following rules will apply to the typing of the date line:

1. Type the date line two lines below the printed letterhead —usually on the fourteenth line.
2. Spell the name of the month in full.
3. Do not use *d*, *nd*, *st*, *th*, or *rd* after the day of the month.
4. The day of the month is separated from the year by a comma.

```
April 18, 19--      October 1, 19--
April 10, 19--
```

INSIDE ADDRESS

The inside address indicates the person—or organization—to whom the letter is directed.

Its position on the page—the number of blank lines to be left between the top of the page and the inside address—depends upon the length of the letter.

The inside address usually contains the following information:

NAME AND/OR TITLE OF THE ADDRESSEE

1. If the name and title are used, separate them by a comma, except the last.

2. If the name and title are so long as to unbalance the other lines, the title should be typed alone on a second line.

```
C. Brown, Esq., Chairman,

C. Brown, Esq.,
Assistant Director,
```

STYLES OF INSIDE ADDRESS

Wherever possible, these details should be restricted to three lines.

Single-line spacing should be used, although the body of the letter may be in double-line spacing.

There are two forms of address—'block' and 'indent'.

In the case of the 'block' method each line begins level with the left-hand margin.

With the 'indent' form the first line begins at the point fixed for the left-hand margin and the other lines five spaces to the right of each preceding line. For short forms of address the indented style is preferable.

The following are examples:

```
Messrs. Stevens & Stockwell,
221 Colchester Avenue,
Brentwood, Essex.

Mrs. J. Adkins,
    11 Bridge Avenue,
        Brighton, 5.
```

(From the 'Dictionary of Typewriting'—Crooks & Dawson)

PERSONAL CORRESPONDENCE

Practice differs in the use of 'Mr.' and 'Esquire' (usually abbreviated as 'Esq.'). However it is best to use 'Esq.', unless specifically told to do otherwise, when addressing correspondents in the U.K. For overseas correspondents, particularly Americans and Canadians, it is preferable to use 'Mr.'.

130

1. Type the company's name exactly as it appears on the firm's letterhead. Do not substitute *and* for & and do not omit the word *The* if it is included in the letterhead.

2. If the name of the company requires an additional line, indent the second line five spaces.

```
Mr.  C.  Brown,  President,
The  Acme  Corporation.

Mr.  C.  Brown,  President,
The  American  Distribution
     &  Supply  Corporation.
```

3. Each line of the inside address should end with a comma, except the last.

BUILDING NUMBER AND STREET NAME

1. Use figures for all building numbers.

2. Use figures for street (avenue, etc.) names above *Ten*.

3. Use cardinal numbers for buildings, but ordinal numbers for streets and avenues.

4. Spell out directions such as *North*, *South*, *East*, and *West*, but sections of the city such as *North-west*, or *South-east* should be abbreviated. In typing these abbreviations, a space after the full stops is optional.

```
Mr.  C.  Brown,  President,
The  Acme  Corporation,
27  Central  Avenue  South,
Worthing,  Sussex.

C.  Brown,  Esq.,
40  Third  Avenue,
Acton,  W.3.
```

131

CITY, DISTRICT AND COUNTY

1. Type the city and district or town and county on one line with a comma between them.
2. If a district number only is used, it is assumed to refer to London.
3. The county should be given, except in the case of major cities in the U.K.

```
Mr. C. Brown, President,
The Acme Corporation,
123 East 45th Street,
New York.

C. Brown, Esq., Chairman,
The Acme Corporation,
85 High Street,
Grantham, Lincs.
```

ATTENTION LINE

The attention line is used to expedite the delivery of the letter to the proper individual or department.

1. The attention line is typed lower than the salutation, centred on the line, and may be underscored.
2. The attention line is used when addressing a company, firm, corporation or government office to locate more easily the interested addressee.

SALUTATION

When a letter is addressed to an individual, the salutation should be directed to that individual. If no name is indicated, you may use any appropriate salutation.

1. Type the salutation at the left margin, two lines below the last line of the inside address or attention line.
2. Names and titles always start with capitals, but not adjectives unless they begin the salutation.

```
Dear Sir,              Dear Mr. Foster,
My dear Sir,           My dear Dr. Jones,
```

The purpose of the subject or 're' line is to give the reader a preview of the contents to be found in the letter without having to read it through completely. Type the subject line two lines below the salutation, centred on the line. (Some firms prefer to have the subject line typed two lines *above* the salutation.)

```
Dear Sirs,
x
Subject: Television Advertising
x
You will be glad to know that Channel
3 is now operating at ---
```

A subject line that requires more than one line may be typed as follows:

```
         Subject: Television Advertising
              Rates as on June 9
```

THE BODY

The message that the letter contains is called the body of the letter. The form in which the body is typed will depend upon the style that is used, but *in all cases*, you must *double space* between each paragraph.

COMPLIMENTARY CLOSE

The complimentary close should express the feeling that the writer wishes to convey. For example, if the salutation is informal, the complimentary close should also be informal.

1. Type the complimentary close two lines below the last line of the body of the letter. (See examples below.)

2. Use an initial capital only for the first word of a complimentary close.

1 The company name is typed two lines below the complimentary close. (See examples below.)

2. It is always typed in capital letters, and spelled out exactly as in the printed letterhead. However, abbreviations are permitted if there is not sufficient space.

3. The company name may be omitted, particularly when using an informal complimentary close, such as *Yours sincerely*. Each firm has its own preferences in this.

DICTATOR'S NAME AND/OR TITLE

1. The dictator's name and/or title is typed four lines below the company name. This allows three blank lines for the signature.

2. The dictator's title may follow his name, with a comma separating them; or the title may be typed directly beneath the name, in which case no punctuation is used after the name.

3. The dictator's name may be omitted and just the title used.

```
x                              x
Yours faithfully,             Yours sincerely,
x                              x
MARTIN ENTERPRISES            MARTIN ENTERPRISES
x                              x
x                              x
x                              x
James Foster,                 Chairman
     Chairman

          x
          Sincerely,
          x
          x
          x
          James Foster
          Chairman
```

134

The reference initials contain the initials of the dictator and the secretary.

1. There may be a space for these allowed in the letterheading.

2. Alternatively they may be typed above the inside address or below the signature. In either case they must be flush with the left-hand margin. They should always appear. If below the signature, they may conflict with the enclosures.

ENCLOSURE NOTATION

To assist the typist or secretary and the person who receives the letter, it is customary to indicate the inclusion of any pieces of literature or other matter with the letter. This notice is the enclosure notation.

1. The enclosure notation is typed flush with the left margin. It may be typed one or two lines below the reference initials.

2. If there is one enclosure, the word *Enclosure*, or *Enc.*, should be used. If there is more than one enclosure, the number of enclosures should follow the reference. Some firms prefer listing each enclosure.

```
Enc.                    Enclosure
Enc. (3)                Enclosures 2

     Enclosures:  Return Envelope
                  Catalogue
```

COPY NOTATION

A letter addressed to one person may be of importance to another individual or group of individuals and copies of the original letter may be sent to these interested parties. In such cases, a notation is made at the bottom of the letter to indicate to the addressee that these copies have been forwarded.

1. Type the copy notation flush with the left margin, two spaces below the reference initials or enclosure notation.

135

2. Special paper is generally used for copy sheets. In such cases, the word 'COPY' is printed on the page. Plain paper may be used with the word 'COPY' typed.

3. The copy notation on the original letter may be indicated as follows:

```
cc Mr. J. Gordon
Copy to The Empire Press, Ltd.
cc: Mr. W. James
c.c. to Mr. A. M. Richards
     Mr. William Young
```

POSTSCRIPT

A postscript is an afterthought that is added to the letter after it has been dictated or typed. It is rarely used in business letters, but every secretary should be familiar with it.

1. The abbreviation *P.S.* is used to identify the postscript.

2. The postscript is typed two lines below the reference initials or below the last notation that is in the letter.

3. It is typed flush with the left margin, but if indented paragraphs are used in the letter, the postscript may also be indented.

```
RES/SL
Enc.
P.S. Your order was sent on April 18.
```